CADOGAN CHESS BOOKS

MASTERING CHESS

A Course in 21 Lessons

CADOGAN CHESS SERIES

Chief Advisor: Garry Kasparov
Editor: Andrew Kinsman

Other popular CADOGAN CHESS books include:

ADAMS/ADAMS
Development of a Grandmaster

AGUR
Bobby Fischer: His Approach to Chess

FORBES
Nigel Short: Quest for the Crown

HODGSON
Chess Travellers Quiz Book

LIVSHITZ
Test your Chess IQ (Books 1–3)

SHEKTMAN
Games of Tigran Petrosian (Volumes 1–2)

SUBA
Dynamic Chess Strategy

VARNUSZ
Paul Keres' Best Games (Volumes 1–2)

VUKOVIC
The Art of Attack in Chess

For a complete catalogue of CADOGAN CHESS books
(which includes the former Pergamon Chess and
Maxwell Macmillan Chess list) please write to:

Cadogan Books, Letts House, Parkgate Road, London SW11 4NQ
Tel: (071) 738 1961
Fax: (071) 924 5491

MASTERING CHESS

A Course in 21 Lessons

by

D. KOPEC, G. CHANDLER

C. MORRISON, N. DAVIES

I. D. MULLEN

CADOGAN CHESS

LONDON, NEW YORK

Cadogan Books
Distribution

UK/EUROPE/AUSTRALASIA/ASIA/AFRICA
Distribution: Grantham Book Services Ltd, Isaac Newton Way, Alma Park Industrial Estate, Grantham, Lincs NG31 9SD. Tel: 0476 67421; Fax: 0476 590223.

USA/CANADA/LATIN AMERICA/JAPAN
Distribution: Macmillan Distribution Center, Front & Brown Streets, Riverside, New Jersey 08075, USA. Tel: (609) 461 6500; Fax: (609) 764 9122.

First published 1985 by Pergamon Press
Reprinted 1986, 1988

First Cadogan Books edition 1994
Reprinted twice 1994

British Library Cataloguing in Publication Data
A catalogue record for this book is available from the British Library.

ISBN 1 85744 062 5

Published by Cadogan Books plc, Letts House, Parkgate Road, London SW11 4NQ

Cover design by Brian Robins

Printed in Great Britain by BPC Wheatons Ltd, Exeter

ACKNOWLEDGEMENTS

The idea for this work originated from discussions with Walter Munn, President of the Scottish Chess Association. The five co-authors are all members of the Edinburgh Chess Masters Association, a group which was formed to supply competent chess tuition for all levels of player ranging from novice to expert. One of the first tasks the group was requested to perform was to produce a teaching package for use by tutors and students in Scotland. It is from that initial project that this present volume has evolved, having undergone several radical changes in the process.

We would like to thank Martin Richardson, former Executive Editor of the Pergamon Chess Series, for his suggestions and help towards the completion of this work. Also, we extend our gratitude to Alistair Girvan, Chairman, S.C.A. Education Sub-Committee; Dr. Ken Stewart, Assistant Secretary, S.C.A.; Bill Wallace, Alec Mac-Farlane, Alec Taylor, Graeme Taylor, Harry Leask, Morag Mullay, Professor D. Michie, the Edinburgh Chess Club and the members of the Machine Intelligence Research Unit for the use of their facilities.

CONTENTS

SYMBOLS

+	check	3 Bb5	a6
+–	White has a winning advantage	4 Bxc6	dxc6
–+	Black has a winning advantage	5 0–0	Bg4
=	equal position	6 h3	h5
0–0	castles king-side	7 hxg4?	hxg4
0–0–0	castles queen-side	8 Nh2	Qh4–+
!	good move	9 f3	g3!
!!	excellent move	0–1	
?	poor move		
??	blunder		
!?	interesting (deserves attention); inviting complications	*Descriptive*	
?!	a dubious move	1 P–K4	P–K4
mate	checkmate	2 N–KB3	N–QB3
1–0	White wins	3 B–N5	P–QR3
0–1	Black wins	4 BxN	QPxB
½–½	drawn game	5 0–0	B–KN5

The following game is given as an example, it is the first 9 moves of a badly played Ruy Lopez (Exchange Variation).

6 P–KR3	P–KR4
7 PxB?	PxP
8 N–R2	Q–R5
Black is winning	
9 P–KB3	P–N6!
White resigns.	

Algebraic

1 e4	e5
2 Nf3	Nc6

Introduction

OUR PURPOSE AND SUGGESTED LEARNING METHODS

DANNY KOPEC, I.M.

In the lessons which follow you will be provided with a great deal of information that is directly or indirectly relevant to every game of chess. The understanding of opening play, the ability to formulate a plan for a position, to analyse its essential components, to carry out a sound combination and finally to use efficient endgame technique to win, is part and parcel of every strong player's technique. However, over the centuries there have been thousands of books written on the game of chess. What, then, is the need for another — especially when none of the subjects covered is particularly original?

We believe that this work is unique in putting five essential chess topics under one cover in a form specially geared towards the club player (graded 1450–1750 [BCF 100–150]). In this regard, one excellent book does come to mind for its broad scope in providing the material necessary for evaluation of almost any chess position: *Point Count Chess* (by Al Horowitz and Geoffrey Mott-Smith). Nevertheless, our work is quite different in that each of its five major subject areas is broken down into four lessons, effectively comprising a 20-lesson course for the serious student whose objective is to become a stronger player. The scenario which leads into a bright discussion of "Tactics and Combinations" is a refreshing yet complete approach to the subject. The elements and principles which guide sound opening play are illustrated by games in three different variations. In "How to Analyse a Position" we consider the methodology for deciding on a particular sequence of moves, based on evaluation of the elements of a position. The endgame and its most knowledge-oriented sub-domains* are considered methodically in Lessons 17–20. In general, the examples chosen throughout are original and recent.

All chess books I have ever come across share in common the approach of attempting to teach or illustrate through examples — either combinations from a given position or complete games — and in this sense ours is no different. However, the good books whose examples have always proven to be the most memorable are those which attach good *labels* to good examples. Take the label of Kotov's in *Think Like a Grandmaster*, "dizziness due to success". This label says a lot in a very few words and is self-explanatory. It is capable of describing the downfall of vain, ignorant, self-confidence in some phase of play better than any other more detailed descriptions — or consider Kmoch's terminology in *Pawn Power in Chess*, "The Sweeper-Sealer-Twist".† Each term in this label has a clear, meaningful, and memorable purpose. Again we try to do the same for you through carefully chosen, concise definitions and examples of many well-known and lesser-known chess terms and concepts.

It has been estimated that the chess master is able to store about 50,000 patterns. No one has as yet attempted to

---

*It is important to have specific information about the theoretical aspects and goals of each of the particular endings discussed. Calculation alone will not suffice, while a little knowledge can go a long way.

†A pawn move which *sweeps* open an outpost square, *seals* an opponent's outpost square, and creates a sudden, possibly unexpected, drastic change in the pawn structure.

ascertain just what these 50,000 patterns inside the head of a chess master are. Perhaps our present understanding of human cognition in terms of perception, memory, and pattern recognition are inadequate to do so. Have no fear, this is also far removed from our aims here, though future developments in artificial intelligence may allow such an endeavour to be feasible.

Our purpose is to provide the serious chess student of middling club strength with the essential elements; the components which comprise the fundamental armoury for good, sound play. Concomitant with these goals is the intention of providing, in a book of about 140 pages, what we consider to be the necessary background for any "cultured" strong player.

During the course of the development of their chess abilities most players find themselves failing or distinctly lacking in knowledge about one phase or another of the game. For most players below master strength the phase where weaknesses appear most often is the endgame. However, many players also often complain about not being able to come up with the appropriate plan for what they evaluate to be a good position, and still more find themselves totally uncomfortable unless the opening follows well-known theoretical paths which they have studied or memorized. This, by necessity, is the clear explanation for and justification of each of the five major sections in this book. Each has its logical place and hopefully readers will find the presentation of material easy to understand and generalize upon, in contrast to, for example, the typical book on a specific opening variation, which tends to overwhelm the reader with great detrimental effects.

The key question is, therefore, will the student be able to *induce* upon the material presented here in order to find correct and creative moves for the positions which arise in his games? That is, if a motif applies for one position with certain features, and the same motif applies for thirty positions with the same features, then perhaps it (or a variant of it) applies for all such positions. In other intellectual endeavours this process could also be called generalization; but, for chess, this alone is not adequate — in that a keen eye for the unique qualities or features of a position must always be present to recognize its requirements. Finding an appropriate plan, such as doubling up on an open file, is still only a small component of the complete, correct conduct of a chess game, which may involve a sequence of associated correct plans. The inductive approach is different and diametrically opposed to the one which provides the examples (i.e. a typical opening monograph) but requires the reader to develop his own ideas by "deduction" (working backwards) from them.

The supplementary lesson on "Practical Tournament Tips and Advice" is intended to give some practical guidelines towards achieving real over-the-board success. The value of *asking questions* (hopefully the right ones) and *learning from one's losses* cannot be overemphasized.

A few words of caution are called for here. Chess is a hard game. There are no easy solutions. Much hard work, persistence and determination is a prerequisite, with no guarantee of excellence or success. This is because chess is unique in having all the ingredients of science, sport, and art. It is not enough to know how, nor is it sufficient to carry out the motions, and likewise for moves with the aesthetic appeal of art for this may nonetheless result in dismal failure. The student who carefully reads all five major sections, who is very knowledgeable, armed with our supplementary Exercises and Practical Tournament Tips and Advice, can unfortunately still be promised nothing in terms of results.

There is no substitute for over-the-board experience of the dynamic element of chess.

You may know all there is to know about opening ideas and principles, about tactics and combinations, about analysis, planning, and even endings, and yet when the moment comes to play the best move (or a good one) you can't do it.

This is where understanding distinguishes itself from information, or even what might be called "knowledge". Experience can play a key role here. The rest is up to you, the reader.

Lessons 1–4

TACTICS AND COMBINATIONS

GEOFF CHANDLER

The Weekend Tournament

Act One

SCENE: *The analysis room at a congress. The players are sitting examining their games. PETE is alone at a chessboard and looking forlorn. JACK enters and sits opposite PETE.*

JACK: "Hi Pete, how did you get on?"

(PETE *looks up and starts moving the pieces about.*)

PETE: "In this position I could have won a piece if I had played this and this."

(PETE *continues moving the pieces about.*)

PETE: ". . . and here I've got a mating attack on. I could have sacrificed my knight on g7, he has to take it, else I win a whole rook! Then I make this neat little quiet move and he can't prevent mate. My opponent showed me that after the game."

JACK: "It's convincing enough, how did you get on?"

PETE: "I lost!"

Curtain

That small scenario is repeated countless times at league and congress post-mortems. The act could have lasted longer, with Jack asking Pete how he missed such things, since he has been playing chess for 15 years now; and Pete replying that he has been busy, felt ill, had a sleepless night, was upset by the traffic and attacked by a swarm of bees!

Pete will always produce excuses for losing games rather than admit that:

(a) He won't play a mating attack involving a sacrifice unless he is 110% sure that it will succeed.

(b) He would dearly love to win opponents' pieces, but never attempts to fathom situations involving a few subtle moves.

LESSON 1

These lessons are for the Petes of the tournament halls.

Before I set about attempting to coat students' arrows with drops of poison, I shall define the terms "tactics" and "combination".

Tactics

This is the term given to the hand-to-hand fighting which takes place on the chessboard when the opposing pieces come into direct contact with each other, i.e. attacking and defending. Basically, a tactical move involves a threat, or a series of threats, to which the opponent must respond immediately. It is normally a forcing sequence, and thus the number of replies is generally limited.

Combination

A combination is a series of tactical moves played in order to gain an advantage (or lessen or neutralize a disadvantage). It may span anything from one to more than fifteen moves.

1

There are four main types of combination:

1. The mating attack.
2. The material gain combination.
3. The positional combination.
4. The drawing combination.

These classifications contain many "tricks of the trade" which form the bulk of all chess players' armoury. A "tactical tree" has been drawn up to aid the student, giving a list of all the main tactical motifs that are discussed here. A good chess move will fall into one of the following three categories:

1. Tactical (as defined above).
2. Strategical (deploying one's forces, following an overall plan, manoeuvring etc.).
3. Forced (getting out of check, recapturing a piece).

It should be noted that mating attack and material gain combinations are closely linked and the ideas used in a material gain combination can be (and very frequently are) used to mate the enemy king.

Positional combinations are played to increase the scope of one's pieces, laying the ground work for a future material gain or mating combination.

Drawing combinations speak for themselves and give the tactically acute player a chance of snatching lost games from the fire.

Tactical Terms

Most of the standard terms are fairly self-explanatory, e.g. obstruction, line-clearing, square-vacating, decoying, etc. In Diagram 1 White uses these four themes to bring about mate.

1 Rd4

The rook sacrifices itself in order to *obstruct* Black's defence of the square h4.

Table 1. A "Tactical Tree" giving a List of Tactical Motifs Found in Combinations

Mating attack	Material gain	Positional	Drawing
Mating patterns	Winning a piece left *en prise*	Creating a passed pawn	Stalemate
Smothered mate		Knight outpost	Perpetual check
Back rank mate	Missing the threat		Reduction to known drawn endings, e.g. two knights and king vs. king, wrong bishop and rook's pawn etc.
King hunt	Knight fork	Rook(s) on the 7th	
Classic bishop sacrifice	Skewers and other forks	Swapping off into a won ending	
Double and discovered check	Pins	Destroying the pawn formation	
Double rook sacrifice	Overworked piece	Taking control of the centre	
Double bishop sacrifice	Desperado piece		
Soft spot attack (any square that is guarded only by a king)	Pawn promotions	Obtaining the two bishops	
	Discovered attack	Forcing a timely queen swap	

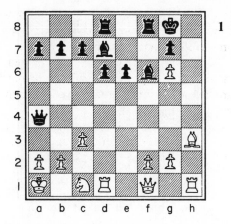

1

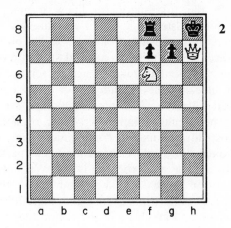

3

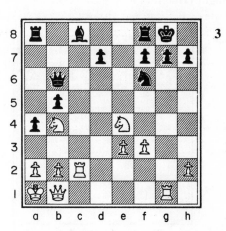

1 ...   **Bxd4**
2 **Bxe6+**

Now the bishop *clears the file* for the rook and queen to use.

2 ...   **Bxe6**
3 **Rh8+**

The rook gives its life to *vacate* h1 for the queen and also to *decoy* the black king on h8, allowing White to gain a vital tempo.

3 ...   **Kxh8**
4 **Qh1+**   **Kg8**

Note that, had White not played 1 Rd4, Black could have defended here with 4 ... Qh4.

5 **Qh7 mate**.

The Mating Attack

Standard Patterns and Thought Processes

"A thorough understanding of the typical mating continuations makes the most complicated sacrificial combinations leading up to them not only not difficult, but almost a matter of course" (Tarrasch).

Just as a cook can imagine the finished version of a meal in preparation, so a chess player must visualize the final mating position or mating pattern which will eventually appear on the board before launching an attack. Let us take first a simple and common mating pattern with queen and knight (Diagram 2).

Now we put more pieces on the board and go back a few moves (Diagram 3).

Since we have given away the mating pattern with queen and knight, it should not take the student long to work out the combination leading to mate:

1 **Rc6!**

This interferes with the queen's protection of the knight on f6 and also clears the b1–h7 diagonal:

1 ...   **dxc6**
2 **Nxf6+**   **Kh8**
3 **Qxh7 mate**.

Looking at it this way, the student may be able to appreciate the apparent paradox that mating attack combinations can be worked out backwards!

In the first place we knew a mating pattern existed, and could visualize giving mate in the position (only the knight on f6 prevented this). So we focused attention on the black knight, found a way to remove it by blocking the defender, and then delivered mate.

Though this example was simple, even the most difficult mating combinations can be broken down into easier component parts. The analogy with cooking is apt. We had a vision of the baked cake in our mind (the mating pattern): we had the ingredients (queen and knight) and the recipe (correct move order).

In the next diagram we see another mating pattern, this time with rook and knight (Diagram 4).

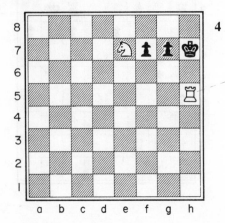

4

Once again we add more pieces and go back a few moves (Diagram 5). The student, once given the mating pattern as a clue, should play out the combination fairly easily.

        1 Ne7+   Kh8
        2 Qxh7+   Kxh7
        3 Rh1 mate.

Yet again, the student can break down the thought process behind the combination. The experienced player will solve

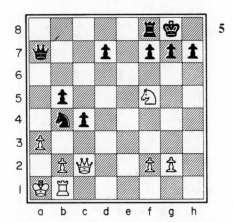

5

similar positions almost without thinking, as such processes have been imprinted on memory and become second nature. The knight can force the black king on to h8. The queen can remove the black h-pawn. Then the rook moves to the h-file when nothing can block the check; it's mate! Broken down like this, it's as easy as . . . baking a cake.

Mating Patterns

(see following diagrams)

The student will note that in all cases a bishop or rook can be replaced by a queen. In the majority of cases using a bishop and rook, neither piece may be in the exact position as shown in the diagram.

In Diagram S mate is forced after 1 f6. Diagram W is a pattern peculiar to queenside castling and the opportunity to play it is not at all rare.

Diagrams X, Y and Z are endgame mating patterns that should be very familiar to the student; Diagram Z, of course, cannot be forced. The student should set these positions up on a board remembering to swap the queen with bishop and rook, as it is usually the queen that delivers the blow. With these positions imprinted on memory circuits, spotting and calculating a mating attack will be much easier.

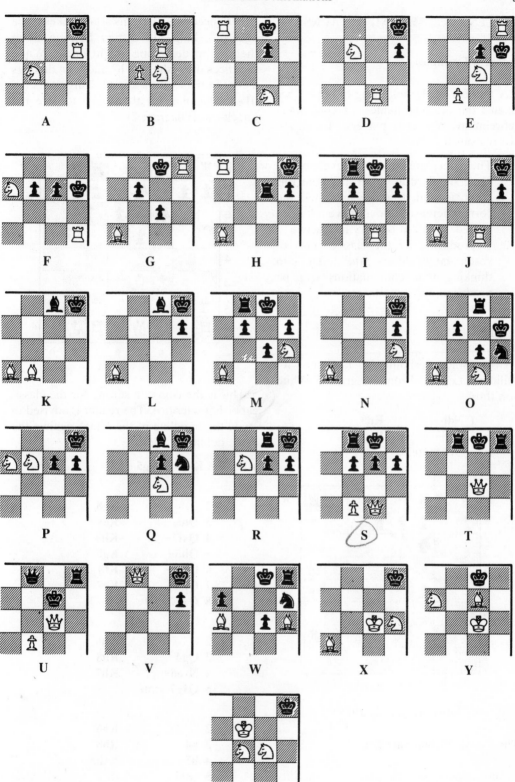

A

B

C

D

E

F

G

H

I

J

K

L

M

N

O

P

Q

R

S

T

U

V

W

X

Y

Z

LESSON 2. MATING ATTACKS

Practical Examples

A number of the following examples are taken from my own games, or encounters between average club players. There are two reasons for this:

1. The games are between players of the same standard as those at whom this book is aimed and sometimes the correct defensive moves have not been played. This can be very instructive.
2. Reproducing all the classic gems of yesteryear would scare the student into thinking that combinations can be produced only by masters.

Smothered Mate

Every student should be familiar with Philidor's Legacy. From Diagram 6 White won thus:

1 Nd6+	Kd8
2 Qe8+	Rxe8
3 Nf7 mate.	

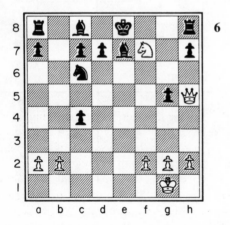

Aitkens–Jacobs 1915

The Classic Bishop Sacrifice

The opportunity to play this sacrifice occurs quite often in games between less experienced players. This attack takes place against a king-side castled position when there is no defending knight on f6. White sacrifices the bishop on h7 and then delivers a check on g5 with a knight. This clears the d1–h5 diagonal for the queen to give the knock-out (Diagram 7).

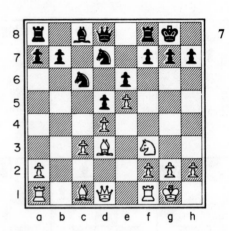

This is the common setting for the classical bishop sacrifice. The reader is advised to study the handling of the attack against the three defensive tries.

1 Bxh7+ Kxh7 2 Ng5+

(a)

2 ...	Kg8
3 Qh5	Re8
4 Qxf7+	Kh8
5 Qh5+	Kg8
6 Qh7+	Kf8
7 Qh8+	Ke7
8 Qxg7 mate.	

(b)

2 ...	Kh6
3 Qg4	Rh8
4 Nxe6+	Kh7
5 Qxg7 mate.	

(c)

2 ...	Kg6
3 h4	Rh8
4 h5+	Rxh5
5 Qd3+	f5
6 exf6+	Kxf6

7	Qf3+	Ke7
8	Qf7+	Kd6
9	Qxh5	

and White wins.

(c1)

3	...	Ndxe5
4	dxe5	Nxe5
5	h5+	Kf6
6	Nh7+	Ke7
7	Ba3+	

White wins.

The keen student will find the classic bishop sacrifice examined in great detail by V. Vukovic in *The Art of Attack in Chess*, published by Pergamon Press.

Double Check

The power of a double check is often a match winner. Its force is the fact that the king must move in reply to a double check. Here is a humorous example from a simultaneous display given by Nimzowitsch (Diagram 8).

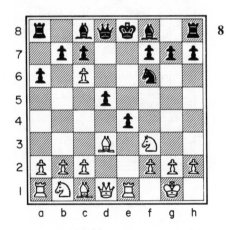

| 1 | Be2 | |

Offering the bait which Black grabs gleefully.

1	...	exf3?
2	cxb7	Bxb7
3	Bb5 double check and mate!	

Discovered Check

This is also a potent weapon. Diagram 9 arose from an off-beat variation of the Ruy Lopez. The player of the white pieces (playing in a minor tournament, Grangemouth 1980) captured the knight on c3 and was lucky to draw. Had he placed more faith in the discovered checks available, he might have found:

1	Nxc6+	Be7
2	Nxe7	Nxd1
3	Ng6!+	Qe7 (forced)
4	Nxe7	Kf8
5	Nxc8 and White is a piece up.	

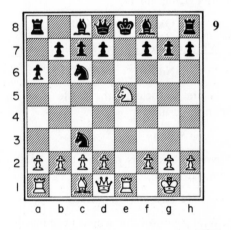

Back Rank Mate

Everybody has been "back rank mated". I once thought for 10 minutes in a comfortable position and allowed a back rank mate next move!

The first example comes from a schoolboy league match. We are about to witness a common blunder — playing the obvious.

White played 1 Rxe5 and resigned after 1 ... Rcxe5, as his intended 2 Qxf7 is now illegal (the queen is pinned). White should have played (Diagram 10):

| 1 | Qxf7+ | Nxf7 |
| 2 | Rxe8 mate. | |

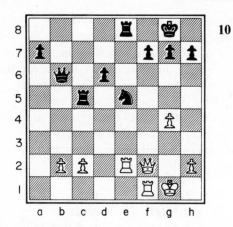

10

The next example comes from the late Vladimir Vukovic. We shall go through it step by step as it contains many tactical motifs (Diagram 11).

1 Qxf8+   Kxf8

White creates the back rank weakness.

2 Nd7+   Bxd7

White self clears the e-file and forces open the c-file.

3 Ba3+   Kg8

Now the king is pushed back behind its own pawns.

4 Rc8+   Bxc8

White exposes the overworked pieces; the bishop is decoyed away from protecting e8.

5 Re8 mate.

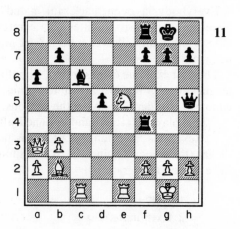

11

The combination is flawless. How can the student be expected to produce finishes like that? We can only recommend keeping your eyes open and developing the habit of examining all captures and forcing sequences as a matter of course.

The Double Rook Sacrifice

The ever-recurring chess battle of material versus development will no doubt rage on till eternity. The double rook sacrifice (where the attacking player leaves both rooks as juicy bait so that the time wasted by the opponent in their capture is used to mate the enemy) speaks loudly for development.

Few examples can match the cheeky imagination of Jacques Mieses, who conjured up a double rook sacrifice shown in Diagram 12.

Mieses played the seemingly pointless Rb8, and his opponent walked into something nasty.

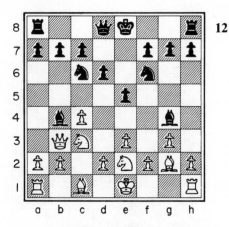

12

Craddock–Mieses

1 ...	Rb8!
2 Ne4	Bc5
3 Nxf6+	Qxf6
4 Bxc6+	bxc6
5 Qxb8+	Kd7
6 Qxh8	

It certainly looks as if Black's 1 ... Rb8 was a blunder.

6 ...	Qf3
7 Kd1	

The only move.

7 ...	Qxe2+
8 Kc2	Qxc4+
9 Kb1	Qd3 mate.

The Double Bishop Sacrifice

This is a fairly rare occurrence in over-the-board play, but the mechanics behind it are worth knowing and can apply to many other typical sacrificial assaults. Here are Tartakower's conditions for the likelihood of the combination being sound:

"The defending king must be exposed and his pieces not readily available for defence. The attacker's rook must serve a double purpose; to prevent the king's escape to the other wing, and to take part in the final assault without any loss of time."

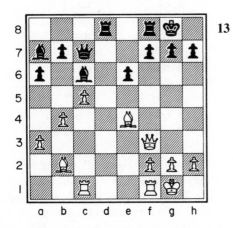

Miles–Browne, Lucerne Olympiad 1982

Diagram 13 is a recent example. Miles finished off with

1 Bxh7+!	Kxh7
2 Qh5+	Kg8
3 Bxg7!	Kxg7

If 3 ... f6 4 Qh8+ Kf7 5 Bxf8 threatens 6 Qh7+

4 Qg5+	Kh8
5 Qf6+	Kg8
6 Rc4!	(1–0)

In effect, the two bishops are fed as cannon-fodder to tear open the king's defences and then the "heavies" (queen and rook) stroll in to deliver a typical mate. The absence of defenders on the king-side is the basis of this and many other violent assaults, including the next example.

The King's Clothes

White has queen, rook, two bishops and knight all within striking distance of the black king. With such an attacking force he can afford to sacrifice a couple of pieces and still have an effective material advantage on the king's wing. The finish is straightforward and brutal (Diagram 14).

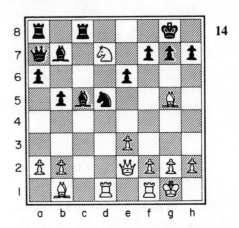

Shestoparov–Serzhanov, USSR 1955

1 Rxd5!	Bxd5
2 Bxh7+	Kxh7
3 Nf6+ with inevitable mate.	

(3 ... gxf6 4 Qh5+ Kg7 5 Qh6+ Kg8 6 Bxf6)

The King Hunt

Here the king is lured or forced out into the open board and then mated. Very often a king hunt combination cannot be fully calculated — the hunter must use "instinct" to judge the outcome.

This is why the chance to play king hunts is often not taken by weaker players, who may lack the courage to sacrifice if they cannot analyse the position fully. A stronger player will sometimes not bother to try to analyse all the possible variations, he will simply know that a king out in the open, at the mercy of an attacker's army, rarely survives (Diagram 15).

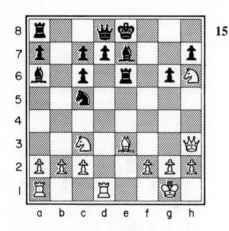

Mullen–Weedon, Edinburgh 1980

1 Nf7	Kxf7
2 Qxh7+	Kf6
3 Bd4+	Kg5

This was as far as White had calculated. He now invested 5 minutes on the clock to finish off with

4 g3

Black can only avoid the threatened 5 Qh4 and 6 Qf4 mate at ruinous cost.

Combinations Against the "Soft Spot"

This is not a particularly new concept in chess strategy, as all players will recognize the term "soft spot" when I remind them that f7 is Black's soft spot at the beginning of the game.

A typical king-side castled position has the square g7 protected only by the king, so this is where Black is often at his weakest.

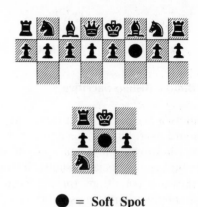

● = Soft Spot

Combinations against f7 are very rare in master games, but there is one line of the Danish Gambit where Black positively invites an attack on this soft spot in order to reduce White's attacking chances:

1 e4	e5
2 d4	exd4
3 c3	dxc3
4 Bc4	cxb2
5 Bxb2	d5
6 Bxd5	Nf6
7 Bxf7+	Kxf7
8 Qxd8	Bb4+
9 Qd2	Bxd2+

with approximately level chances, though nobody seems quite sure about this position.

The chance to play combinations against f7 (or f2 if White is careless) crops up more frequently in games between less-experienced players. The opening lessons in this manual, plus the player's own experience, should be sufficient acquaintance with the necessary preconditions, as most combinations against an uncastled king are now well-known opening traps. I give two examples from less familiar settings.

The first is a "what could have happened" between two players renowned for their fiery attacks.

Alekhine–Marshall

1	d4	Nf6
2	c4	e6
3	Nf3	Ne4
4	Nfd2	Bb4

"a typical Marshall trap" (Alekhine).

Alekhine played 5 Qc2 and won convincingly. Had he chosen the natural looking "Sunday morning move" (5 a3?) then he would have found himself with a lost game after 5 ... Qf6.

The square f7 can also be a target in a safe looking castled position. Here is a typical "bolt from the blue" combination which could equally well be categorized under the back rank section.

McNab–Mullen

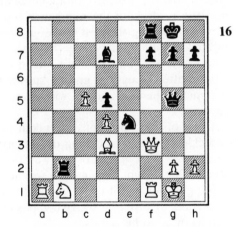

16

1 ...		Bg4?

Not reckoning on

2	Qxf7!+

when Black fell off his chair, then resigned.

The Soft Spot at g7

By playing natural developing moves, a player can lock on to the soft spots f7 and h7 fairly easily with king's bishop, knight and queen.

The real soft spot in a castled position is g7 (or g2). However, it is not all that easy

for the white pieces to focus on this square, and generally it is necessary to spend more time co-ordinating pieces in order to overpower it.

In some main line variations of the Ruy Lopez it is not uncommon to see the white queen's knight hop all over the board to reach f5 and eye g7, i.e. Nb1–d2–f1–e3/g3, and then on to f5. Only the queen's bishop can hit g7 using straightforward development (a fianchetto or, in some cases, Bh6). This is one reason why castled kings tend to live longer than kings who stay in the centre; g7 is harder to hit than f7.

A gathering of strength against g7 normally spells the end (Diagram 17).

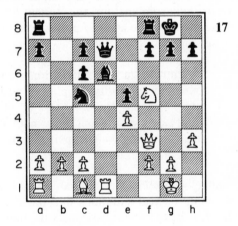

17

Capablanca–Corio

The knight is a tower of strength on f5 and a simple piece count of attackers and defenders around the black king gives a hint of the coming disaster.

1	Bh6!	Ne6
2	Bxg7	Nf4

If 2 ... Nxg7, 3 Qg4 f6 4 Nh6+ wins the queen.

3	Bxe5	Ng6
4	Nh6 mate.	

A word of warning: Don't waste time on the clock looking for mates that don't exist! You can't will a position to contain a combination. The student *must* play over typical mating attacks and sacrificial combinations in order to build up a "chess instinct". The types of positions which contain the seeds for such combinations will soon begin to be recognized. Also, it should then be easier to produce attacking games and find the most aggressive squares for pieces.

A mating combination is normally the easiest of the four main types of combination to play! Even a crude computer can work out a difficult mate in six if all the moves are forced. With checkmate the game ends. The student need not calculate past mate. (Though it may be necessary to anticipate a left hook from the opponent.) But when playing a material gain, positional or drawing combination, the student has to have the ability to assess a position that will arise some moves ahead.

> "A knowledge of combinations is the foundation of positional play. This is a rule which has stood its test in chess history and one which we cannot impress forcibly enough upon the young chess-player" (Reti).

Calling yourself a "positional player" and avoiding tactical situations like the plague for fear of the ability to cope with them is doing nothing but fooling yourself. As encouragement for the student, we mention that tactical ability is one chess skill which may improve dramatically with study. Reti again:

> "It is a mistake to think that combination is solely a question of talent and cannot be acquired. The same elements, as double-attacks, pins, obstructions etc., occur here again and again in more or less complicated associations. The more one sees of them, the easier it becomes to conceive and follow through such combinations by oneself."

Test Positions

In all the following positions (Diagrams 18–29) the player to move has a forced mate on the board. Some of the solutions are rather lengthy and this should convince the student that the difficulty of a combination has little to do with the number of moves involved. Finding the best move in a complicated position may be beyond the greatest players, but finding a forced mate in 9 can often be easy — given a knowledge of typical themes and a willingness to calculate.

A few of these positions are taken from Locock's excellent (and long out of print) *Imagination in Chess*. Locock was of the opinion that imagination in chess was not an innate gift, but that it could be taught, and proceeded to prove it by giving positions such as these to his pupils.

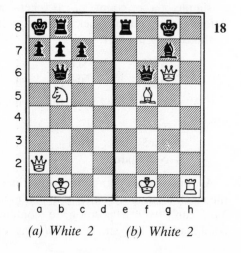

(a) White 2   *(b) White 2*

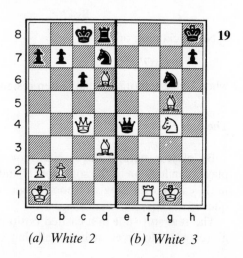

(a) White 2   *(b) White 3*

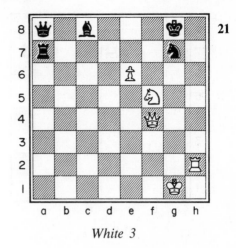

White 3

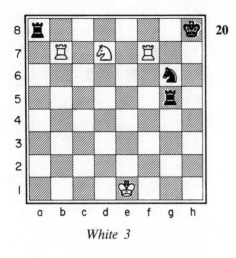

White 3

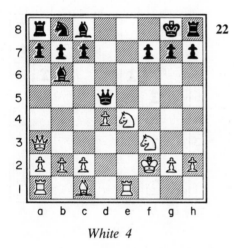

White 4

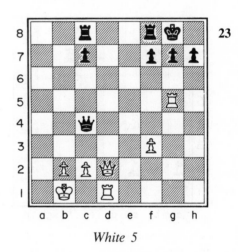

White 5

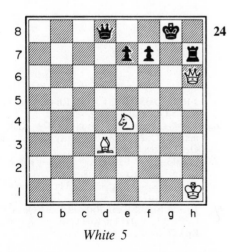

White 5

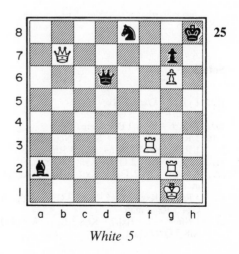

White 5

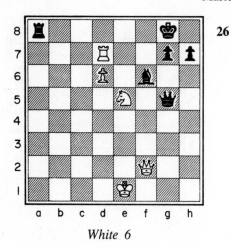

White 6   **26**

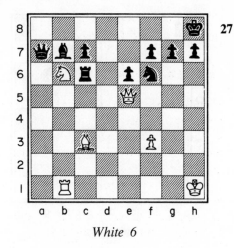

White 6   **27**

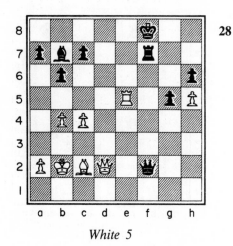

White 5   **28**

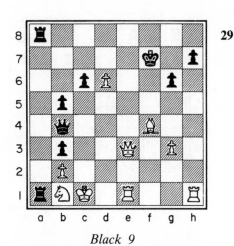

Black 9   **29**

Solutions

18a.   1 Qxa7+ Qxa7 2 Nxc7 mate.

18b.   1 Rh8+ Kxh8 2 Qh7 mate.

19a.   1 Qxc6+ bxc6 2 Ba6 mate.

19b.   1 Rf8+ Nxf8 2 Bf6+ Kg8 3 Nh6 mate.

20.   1 Rh7+ Kxh7 2 Nf6+ Kh6 3 Rh7 mate.

21.   1 Ne7+ Rxe7 2 Qf8+ Kxf8 3 Rh8 mate.

22.   1 Nf6+ gxf6 2 Qf8+ Kxf8 3 Bh6+ Kg8 4 Re8 mate.

23.   1 Rxg7+ Kxg7 2 Qg5+ Kh8 3 Qf6+ Kg8 4 Rg1+ Qg4 5 Rxg4 mate.

24.   1 Nf6+ exf6 2 Bxh7+ Kh8 3 Bg6+ Kg8 4 Qh7+ Kf8 5 Qxf7 mate.

25.   1 Rf8+ Qxf8 2 Rh2+ Kg8 3 Rh8+ Kxh8 4 Qh1+ Kg8 5 Qh7 mate.

26.   1 Rd8+ Rxd8 (1 ... Bxd8 2 Qf7+ Kh8 3 Qf8 mate) 2 Qa2+ Kh8 3 Nf7+ Kg8 4 Nh6+ Kh8 5 Qg8+ Rxg8 6 Nf7 mate.

27.   1 Qxf6 gxf6 2 Bxf6+ Kg8 3 Rg1+ Kf8 4 Nd7+ Ke8 5 Rg8+ Kxd7 6 Rd8 mate.

28.   1 Qd8+ Kg7 2 Rxg5+ hxg5 3 h6+ Kxh6 4 Qh8+ Rh7 5 Qxh7 mate.

29.   1 ... Rxb1+ 2 Kxb1 Ra1+ 3 Kxa1 Qa4+ 4 Kb1 Qa2+ 5 Kc1 Qa1+ 6 Kd2 Qxb2+ 7 Kd3 Qc2+ 8 Kd4 Qc4+ 9 Ke5 Qd5 mate.

LESSON 3. MATERIAL GAIN COMBINATIONS

Leaving a Piece *En Prise*

Only the rawest recruits to our noble game unwittingly leave pieces on attacked squares. This section deals with leaving a piece hanging in plausible positions (Diagram 30).

The most common cause is the pawn grab. White plays a harmless looking couple of opening moves; Black, feeling his opponent is reluctant to fight, steals a pawn. The rest is history. The opening moves:

1 e4	e5
2 Nf3	d6
3 c3	Nf6
4 Be2	Nxe4?
5 Qa4+	

and picks up the knight on e4.

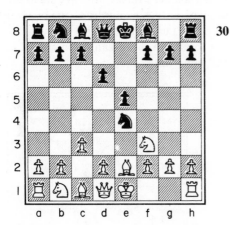

Missing the Threat

"What's my opponent up to?" is a question which should be asked after every move, even if you are in the middle of a forcing sequence. By studying positions where blunders have occurred, the student will build up an automatic alarm system. Bells will ring, lights will flash and memory cells will scream. (Also, there is a lot to be said for a good night's sleep before an important game.)

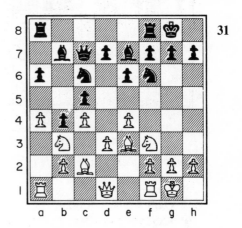

Todd–Chandler 1982

1 ...	Ng4?!

Setting a diabolical trap.

2 Bxc5?	Bxc5
3 Nxc5	Nd4

Discovers an attack on the knight and threatens 4 ... Nxf3+ and mate on h7.

4 g3	Nxc2
5 Nxb7?!	

The desperado knight cannot match his black counterpart.

5 ...	Nxa1
0–1.	

The Double Attack

A double attack is really a fork in an elaborate setting. In Diagram 32 as White I was the exchange up and looking to bring matters to a head. I could see a distant threat for my opponent using the rook on g6 against my king. I allowed him to play a "combination" winning a pawn and opening up my king position. I had looked deeper into the position and found a double attack that forced immediate resignation.

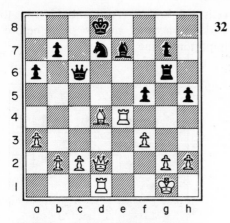

Chandler–Austin, Edinburgh 1977

1 Qa5+	b6
2 Qxf5	Rxg2+
3 Kxg2	Qxc2+
4 Bf2	Qxd1

All according to plan, thought my opponent.

5 Rd4   1–0

With mate or loss of the queen.

The Discovered Attack

Diagram 31 is a good example of a discovered attack. Diagram 33 has a discovered attack as its main theme, but also features a curious case of "chess blindness". White had played his pawn to a3 to prevent any bishop checks on b4, and under this illusion played as follows.

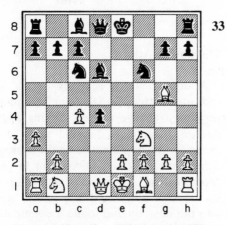

Girvan–Chandler, Edinburgh 1980

1 Nxd4??

Here I must confess I felt like a forgetful fisherman who could not remember where he placed his lobster pots. I was sure that pawn was poisoned . . . then sanity prevailed.

1 ...	Nxd4
2 Qxd4	

Now the discovered attack on the queen.

2 ...	Bb4+
3 Qd2	Bxd2+
	0–1

The Overworked Piece

Chess pieces are lazy; they hate having defending duties, but tolerate them as a necessity. However, should you designate too many defending duties to one single piece, then its claim for more pay can be heard all over the board. We have already seen a perfect example of an overworked piece in Diagram 11. The theme is always the same, no piece can be in two places at the same time.

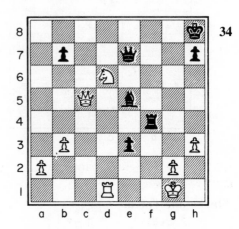

Tajmanov–N.N., USSR 1978

1 Nf5!

White introduces back rank mate threats. The black queen is protecting both back rank and bishop.

(a)

1 ...	Qxc5
2 Rd8+	Qf8
3 Rxf8 mate.	

(b)

1 ...	e2
2 Rd8+	Qxd8
3 Qxe5+	mating.

(c)

1 ...	Qe8
2 Qxe5+	Qxe5
3 Rd8+	mating.

The Desperado

This is a piece which is about to be captured, but whilst still alive will sell its life as dearly as possible. On the section covering "soft spots" we saw a "desperado queen" in the Danish Gambit. White played 9 Qd2 (for the bishop) and restored material equality. Diagram 35 is by A.R.B. Thomas.

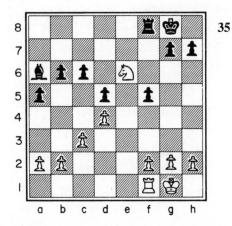

35

Here we see two potential desperados selling their lives for pawns.

1 Nxf8	Bxf1
2 Nxh7	Bxg2

The bishop tries to match the display of suicidal tendencies shown by the knight.

3 Nf6+	Kf7

If 3 ... gxf6, 4 Kxg2 and White wins the ending.

4 Nd7	Be4
5 Nxb6	

and both desperados survive, but White's has caused more damage and created a winning ending.

The Knight Fork

Here is a nice piece of play with the knight supplying the sting in the tail.

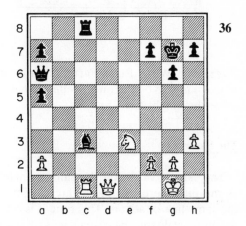

36

Henley–Matko 1982

1 Rxc3	Rxc3
2 Qd4+	Qf6

The move that Black thought White had missed, but it's all part of the plan to set up a geometrical formation for the knight fork.

3 Qxf6+	Kxf6
4 Nd5+	
	1–0

Pins

Diagram 37 occurred in an Edinburgh league match. I don't remember the players, but I did witness this.

1 Ba5	b6??

Underestimating the pin, or simply not seeing it.

2 Bc3	

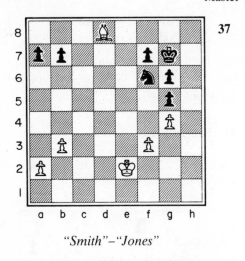

"Smith"–"Jones"

Zugzwang. When Black eventually ran out of pawn moves on the queen-side, he had to leave the knight to its fate.

The Skewer

The skewer works on the same principle as the pin where two pieces are caught on the same line of action. This time it is often the more valuable piece which is attacked and forced to move; allowing a less (or equally) valuable piece to be captured. The skewer is sometimes referred to as an x-ray attack. It is the king that is, usually, the primary target in a skewer.

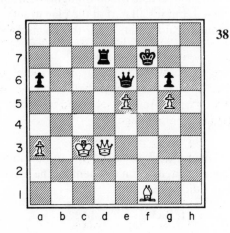

White gives Black an unpleasant choice. Have the queen pinned to the king, or be skewered.

1	Qxd7+!	Qxd7
2	e6+	

if 2 ... Qxe6, 3 Bc4 is the pin, and if

2	...	Kxe6
3	Bh3+	

is the skewer, and White draws what looked like a difficult ending.

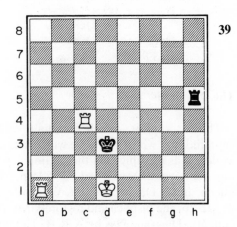

Diagram 39 shows a famous study by Stamma.

Black has a couple of threats — Kxc4 and Rh1 mate.

1 Rh4!

Threatening 2 Ra3 mate.

1	...	Rxh4
2	Ra3+	K-any
3	Ra4+	wins

The rook on h4 is skewered.

Pawn Promotions

Combinations of this type are always in the air when a foot-soldier reaches the 6th or 7th rank. The student should build up a repertoire of pawn promotion tricks for future use. The following three will serve as a good base.

1 Rf8+

White deflects the king.

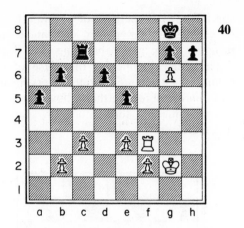

40

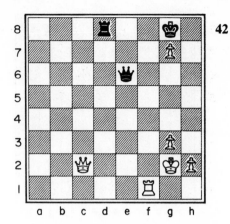

42

1 ...   Kxf8
2 gxh7 and wins.

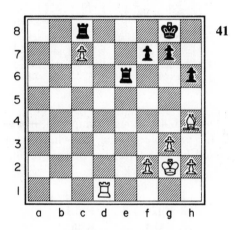

41

Diagram 41 shows a simple setting which gives a ploy worth knowing.

1 Rd8+   Re8

This defence is usually sufficient but

2 Rxe8+   Rxe8
3 Bd8 and wins.

Diagram 42 is an example showing one of the many *under promotion* tricks.

1 Rf8+   Rxf8
2 Qh7+   Kxh7
3 gxf8=N+ and wins.

The Positional Combination

In a pure positional combination no material is gained, but the scope of one's pieces should be increased. The need to play a positional combination usually comes when a player has other advantages that cannot be maintained. Let us suppose, for example, that a player has a lead in *development* and *space*, but can find no way to construct a mating attack (perhaps due to an early exchange of queens and a couple of minor pieces). Another train of thought, or strategy, looking for the seed of a material gain combination may also be fruitless if the opponent has left no targets to attack.

Advantages in development and space tend to disappear if not cashed in right away, so the player must seek some other way of keeping the initiative and not allow the opponent into the game.

In Diagram 43 White trades a lead in space and development for a couple of active rooks. (Active rooks tend to lead to a permanent advantage).

1 Nxd7   Bxd7
2 Bh7+   Kxh7
3 Rxd7

Play could continue

3 ...   Rac8
4 Re1

Followed by Ree7 with a huge plus for White.

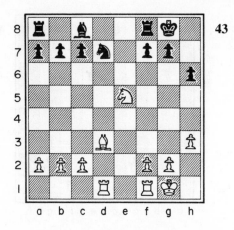

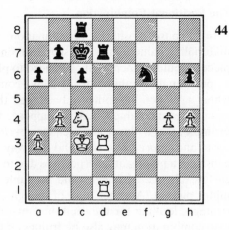

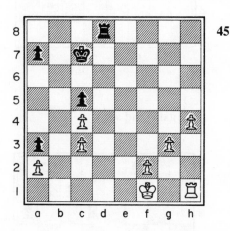

special case of repetition of position, is one of them. Neither player can make any progress, the game is abandoned as a draw.

The other lifeline is "the curse of the clumsy" — stalemate. I'm sure everyone has had that awful feeling that follows throwing a won game out the window by allowing stalemate.

Diagram 45, though composed, is a wonderful example of the half-chances often missed by inexperienced players tending a lost position. Black plays:

1 ...	Rd1+
2 Kg2	Rxh1
3 Kxh1	Kb6

White can only watch as the black king buries himself with king a5–a4 and then plays pawn a5 = stalemate.

Opposite coloured bishops, the wrong bishop and the rook pawn, and two knights vs. king are all saving clauses worth knowing.

Diagram 46, again a composition, is a beautiful example of the art of saving a lost game.

1 Ra1	Kg2
2 Kh8!	Bf1
3 Ra7	h1=Q (or R)+
4 Rh7	Qg1
5 Rg7+	

½–½

In Diagram 44 White simplifies the main advantage, the king-side majority, into a win.

1 Rxd7+	Nxd7
2 Rxd7+	Kxd7
3 Nb6+	Kd8 (or Kc7)
4 Nxc8	Kxc8
5 g5 and wins.	

E.g. **5 ... hxg5 6 h5! wins.**
5 ... Kd8 6 gxh6 wins.
5 ... h5 6 g6 wins.

The Drawing Combination

The title speaks for itself — the combining player is trying to save a lost game. The laws of chess aid the losing player by giving a couple of lifelines. Perpetual check, a

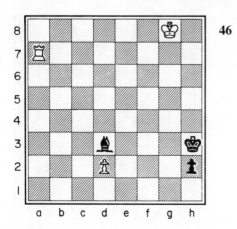

Perpetual Check

This drawing device (the perpetual nuisance) saved a lost game I was tending in the following position from an allegro tournament.

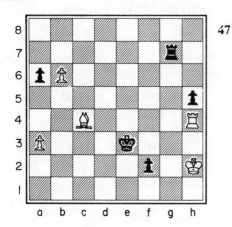

47

Deacon–Chandler, Alnwick 1979

| 1 ... | f1=Q!? |

The drowning man clutches at straws. It was now or never while I still had some bait to offer.

| 2 Bxf1 | Kf2 |
| 3 Bxa6? | |

3 Bh3 or 3 Rf4+ wins.

| 3 ... | Rg2+ |

And Black carries on checking at g1–g2–g3.

½–½

Opposite Coloured Bishops

The reader should beware that the rule of thumb "opposite coloured bishops always draw" is tainted. Let us say that if an opposite coloured bishop endgame can be won, it will be only after surmounting technical difficulties.

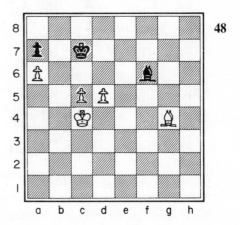

48

Diagram 48, an analysis by Mednis, is an example of a frustrating drawn ending.

| 1 ... | Be7! |
| 2 d6+ | |

If 2 Kd4 Bf6+, 3 Ke4 Be7 4 c6 Bd6 and the bishop stays on the a3–f8 diagonal preventing progress.

| 2 ... | Bxd6 |
| 3 cxd6+ | Kxd6 |

And although White has the "correct" bishop for the rook's pawn, the black king reaches b8 and cannot be dug out of the corner.

½–½.

LESSON 4. INSTRUCTIVE POSITIONS AND CONSTRUCTIVE ADVICE

I hope you can add more strings to your bow by studying the following positions and games. Tactics form a large part of the successful club players' armoury. Here is a selection of mistakes typical of average club players (Diagram 49).

Accepting the Obvious (part one)

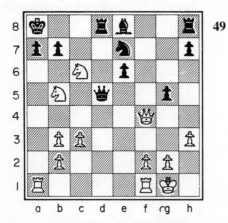

Chandler–Austin 1980

Black spent 5–10 minutes looking for ways to stop mate at both a7 and c7. There are three different mating patterns.

1 ...	Nxc6
2 Nc7+	Kb8
3 Na6+	Ka8
4 Qb8+	R or Nxb8
5 Nc7 mate.	

1 ...	bxc6
2 Rxa7 mate.	

1 ...	a6
2 Nc7 mate.	

I spent the time praying to every god I knew. My opponent resigned(?). With

1 ...	Qxg2+!
2 Kxg2	Bxc6+
3 Qf3	Bxf3+

he could at least have drawn.

Accepting the Obvious (part two)

Diagram 50 arose in a correspondence match, Scotland v. Austria. White has just captured a knight on d4. The threat is:

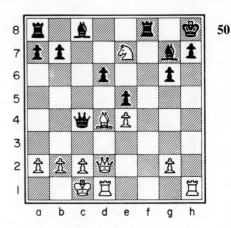

Chandler–Parker

18 Rxh7+	Kxh7
19 Rh1+	Bh6
20 Qxh6 mate.	

The postman brought me a nice surprise. Black resigned! He can play:

17 ...	Bg4!

and not only save the game, but win in many variations, e.g.

18 Rxh7+	Kxh7
19 Rh1+	Bh5
20 g4(?)	Rf1+
and Black wins.	

Don't over-estimate your opponent's attacking chances. Remain cool in defence, and look at *all* moves, no matter how crazy they may at first appear.

DON'T BE A LIPSCHUETZ

In other words, don't sweep your losses or tactical oversights under the carpet. It is a good idea to invest some time in studying your errors. If you keep missing tactical combinations game after game then you must take time out to sharpen your claws. Diagram 51 shows how White missed the following win:

1 Qh8+	Kxh8
2 Rf8 mate.	

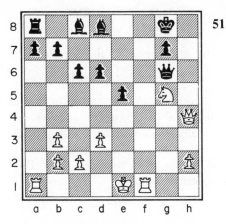

Lipschuetz–Zukertort

O.K., you might forgive him. Everyone makes oversights like that. But . . .

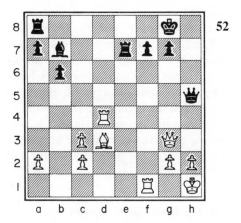

Lipschuetz–Lasker

Diagram 52 shows how White missed the same sort of decoying combination. He should have played:

1 Rh4	Q anywhere
2 Rh8+	Kxh8
3 Qh3+	Kg8
4 Qh7+	

and mate next move.

There is nothing worse than sitting in the analysis room looking for sympathy over a missed win. Nobody wants to know.

Tactical Foresight

Correct calculation is a necessity for any type of combination. However, what is often more important is the ability to assess the position which will arise after the combination has been played. Sometimes there may lurk a nasty counter-combination not seen by either player till the position clarifies. On other occasions there may be a twist in the tail. Diagram 52 is a perfect example. The position is composed from a variation of a game I played.

It certainly looks as if White has a potential knight fork on c7. White can decoy the queen to a8 and knock-out the guard on e6. That seems simple enough. We then only have to calculate if the white king and knight can halt Black's king-side pawns. Once again there seems to be no problem. The black e-pawn will be doubled, the knight can pick up the c-pawn via b6, then blockade the e-file. The white king can catch the h-pawn once Black has created a passed pawn. Play continues (Diagram 53):

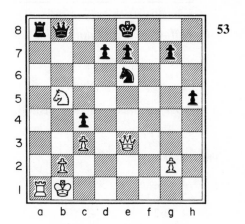

1 Rxa8	Qxa8
2 Qxe6	dxe6
3 Nc7+	Kd7
4 Nxa8	

The "combination" is now complete; White can look forward to an early Black retirement.

4 ...	**Kc6!**

Oops! the white knight is lost and Black wins the ending easily. Always try to look just one move deeper.

The Lazy Move

Diagram 16 was an example of the lazy move (1 ... Bg4?). In this example the play leading to the blunder contains many tactical motifs already discussed (Diagram 54).

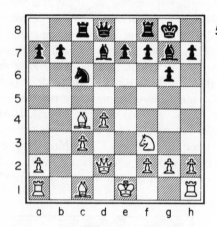

Ratcliff–Chandler, Edinburgh 1979

1 ...	**Nxd4**

A *discovered attack* on the bishop.

2 Bxf7+

The *desperado*.

2 ...	**Rxf7**
3 Nxd4	**Qc7**
4 Bb2	**e5**
5 Ne2	**Rd8**

Threatening a *discovered attack* on the queen:

6 Rd1

Pinning the bishop:

6 ...	**Rff8**

Easing the *pin* and renewing the threat.

7 Qd5+	**Kh8**
8 Qd6??	

The *lazy move* 8 Qb3 was correct.

8 ...	**Ba4!**

Discovers a *double attack* on the queen, *skewers* a rock under *double attack*, threatens an *x-ray mate* in one. The American Grandmaster Lombardy understandably refers to such moves (8 ... Ba4!) as bone crushers!

0–1.

Ideas in Action

The following short tactical games will give the student the chance to see in action some of the tactical terms and ideas I have discussed.

You should never miss the chance to play over any miniature (any game less than 25 moves). Such games usually contain useful tactical ideas that can be reproduced in your own games. Some players with intermediate grades refrain from clashing with their opponents in the early stages, but if an opening error is not punished immediately, either by tactical or positional means, then it may turn out to be a good move!

Learning from Short Games

Some time in the past I played out the following three opening traps. (In my beginner days I filled note books with every opening trap and short game I could lay my hands on.) Without this tactical background I would certainly have missed a lot of sacrificial chances that have happened my way over the years.

1 e4	e5
2 Nc3	Nf6
3 Bc4	Nxe4
4 Qh5	Nd6
5 Bb3	Nc6
6 d4	exd4
7 Nd5	g6?

8	Qe2+	Be7
9	Nf6+	Kf8
10	Bh6 mate.	

1	e4	e5
2	Nf3	Nc6
3	Nc3	Bb4
4	Bc4	Nf6
5	0-0	d6
6	Nd5	Bc5
7	d3	Bg4
8	c3	Ne7?
9	Nxf6+	gxf6
10	Nxe5	Bxd1
11	Bxf7+	Kf8
12	Bh6	mate.

1	e4	Nf6
2	Nc3	d5
3	exd5	Nxd5
4	Nge2	Bg4
5	g3?!	Nc6
6	Bg2	Ne5
7	Bxd5?	Qxd5
8	Nxd5	Nf3+
9	Kf1	Bh3 mate.

or

8	0-0	Nf3+
9	Kh1	Ng5+
10	Nxd5	Bf3+
11	Kg1	Nh3 mate.

The linking theme was the bishop going to h6 or h3 giving mate.

Chandler–Gillain, Edinburgh 1981, Four Knights

1	e4	e5
2	Nf3	Nc6
3	Nc3	Bc5(?)

White can gain a positional plus with the "fork trick" 4 Nxe5, but I took a chance and waited for a bigger opportunity. One came, but I very easily could have been chasing a lost game for not jumping on Black immediately.

4	Bb5	d6
5	0-0	Bg4
6	d3	Nf6
7	Bg5	Bxf3?

White had been playing lazy moves up to here, but Black lets him gain the advantage with this unprovoked exchange. 7 ... h6 was better.

8	Qxf3	a6
9	Nd5!?	axb5

I had now intended 10 Nxf6+ gxf6 11 Bxf6 picking up the rook. Suddenly the alarm bells rang and I spotted he could play 11 ... Nd4! in answer to my 11 Bxf6. Average players tend to miss opponent's threats but find moves like 11 ... Nd4! when their back is against the wall. A knowledge of how the casual and weak club players react in tactical situations certainly benefits the student. My only hope was to leave him alone for a move so as not to force him to find the best continuation! Then the bishop and knight mating pattern, like a voice from the past, came into my head.

10	c3	Ne7
11	Qxf6!	gxf6
12	Nxf6+	Kf8
13	Bh6 mate.	

Lucky? Yes! But I had gambled on him wanting to break the pin on his knight. 0-0 lost to 11 Nxf6+. 10 c3 tempted a natural-looking move. I should like to say that I would have found 11 Qxf6! without knowing or remembering the previous examples, but that would not be honest.

In the next example we shall concentrate on what never happened, rather than what did. White misses a win that anybody would have been proud of — the point being that anybody with a little tactical know-how could have produced it.

Johnson–Hayman, Edinburgh 1981, Scotch Game

1	e4	e5
2	Nf3	Nc6
3	d4	exd4
4	Nxd4	Nxd4?
5	Qxd4	d6
6	Bc4	c6
7	Nc3	Ne7

Black's opening play leaves a lot to be desired; however, it is only the following tactics which interest us.

8 Bg5   Qb6

I was watching this game (a league match), and I shook my head in sympathy as White played 9 Qxb6. White eventually lost a long ending. "Why not take the pawn on d6?" I asked after the game.

9 Qxd6

"I was worried about 9 ... Qxb2" came the reply.

9 ...   Qxb2

White's analysis stopped here and he did not like what he saw. However, anyone who has taken the time (a few very entertaining evenings) to play out the "Golden Oldies", or has studied opening traps, would know that Black cannot waste as much time in the opening as he has done here. Linking a few tricks together, I demonstrated the following line of play. (The black moves were played by the player of the white pieces in the original game.)

10 Rd1	**Qxc3+**
11 Bd2	**Qxc4**
12 Qd8+	**Kxd8**
13 Ba5+	**Ke8**
14 Rd8 mate.	

To miss such a beautiful win and then go on to lose is a common failing amongst weaker players. *There is a cure*! A good dose of Morphy, washed down with a couple of hours studying tactics.

In this next example, which is not an untypical league match between two players of intermediate grade, we see one player sacrifice (in dubious circumstances) for what he believes to be compensation (two pawns and an exposed king for a bishop). On his next turn, the sacrificing player makes a "lazy" move and loses a piece. The defending player then proceeded to swap pieces, which is usually correct when one is material ahead, but in doing so only furthered the

attacker's development. The defending player should have considered a counter-sacrifice and then used his extra piece to bring about a "technique" win.

As the game progressed, the defender panicked and tried to rush his king to the queen-side. White remained cool and played a fairly easy queen sacrifice when three pieces down! Suddenly the game was over. The moral of this game is: when material ahead, you should always look for the most aggressive way of giving it back. Getting a won position can be very easy, actually winning the game is the hard part!

G. Chandler–Dr. Ratcliff, Edinburgh 1983, Evans Gambit

1 e4	**e5**
2 Nf3	**Nc6**
3 Bc4	**Bc5**
4 b4	**Bb6**
5 b5	**Na5**
6 Bxf7+?!	

Two central pawns and an exposed king for a piece is playable compensation.

6 ...	**Kxf7**
7 Nxe5+	**Kf8**
8 0–0	

but this very embarrassing blunder, played after 5 seconds' thought, should have given Black an easy win.

8 ...	**Bd4**
9 Ba3+	**d6**
10 c3	**Bxe5**
11 f4	**Bf6**
12 e5	**Be7**
13 Qe2	**Bf5**
14 g4	

White has no choice, he must keep up some form of momentum.

14 ...	**Bxb1**
15 Raxb1	**d5**
16 Bc1	**Ke8?**

6 ... d4!, giving his pieces more room, was far better.

| 17 | d4 | Nc4 |
| 18 | f5 | Bg5? |

Black's policy of swapping off pieces when material ahead is usually correct, but after my next move his position becomes very difficult.

19	f6!	Bxc1
20	fxg7	Be3+
21	Qxe3!	

White, three pieces down, sacrifices the queen. If 21 ... Nxe3, 22 Rf8+ ... 23 Rxd8 and gxh8.

21	...	Qe7
22	gxh8=Q	Nxe3
23	Qxg8+	Kd7
24	e6+	

Wrapping it up neatly before any more blunders.

24	...	Qxe6
25	Qxe6+	Kxe6
26	Rbe1	
	1–0.	

Motivation to Study

Nothing is more tedious than setting and resetting different positions up on the chessboard. After you have spent 10 minutes studying the tactical ins and outs of a position, you have to destroy it and painstakingly reset another.

After three or four such positions you start to waste your time by trying to solve positions from diagrams. If you're just starting off on the road of chess study, then this exercise is a complete waste of time.

Strong players may solve diagrammed positions within seconds. Some, Bronstein, for example, even prefer to analyse on the demonstration board. However, when these players were at your stage they set and reset instructive positions on a chessboard. How can you ask your memory cells and imagination to construct a mating net or produce a subtle manoeuvre if they have never seen it before?

You don't play chess on chessboards the size of diagrams, yet students of the game will spend an hour or more solving positions from a book or magazine without the aid, or the proper use, of a set. Consequently, when they sit down to reproduce their skills, they find a mental block in some positions and labour to carry off elementary attacking methods. Give them the same position on a diagram and they find even the most difficult moves!

To aid in calculation, positions must be set up on a standard size board so that certain patterns are formed in the mind. The eye is trained at flowing along diagonals and files, instead of being fixed on a 1½-inch square.

I was given this advice many years ago by a strong player after I had asked him how to improve my analysis. I owe him a lot. Players will find a marked improvement in their play if they take the time to study with the weapon they fight with, a standard sized set.

I'm fairly certain about the "diagram syndrome". On a journey from Glasgow, I armed myself with a *CHESS* magazine to kill time. From the six "winning combinative play" positions I had only one right! I rarely study, or even try to solve, problems without a set and board, but on this occasion I did not have one. That night I dug out some really old *CHESS* magazines and with the aid of a set . . . 18 out of 18 correct!

Summary

I once read, in a very old chess book, "Both players are reminiscent of two old sea captains, trying to manoeuvre their huge galleons into a position to deliver a broadside." You can liken all chess players to such captains in command of men-of-war.

There is the absolute beginner who usually gets sunk before leaving the harbour (entering the middle-game) or else runs aground.

The weak club player normally runs out of shot (no ideas) and is becalmed, drifting towards the rocks (mated without resistance).

Then there is the semi-skilled player who has a reasonable gun crew (tactical ability), but terrible navigators (positional sense) and cannot move into a position to get a good shot. They have been known to sink the occasional prize, but usually it is a case of being out-manoeuvred and collecting a full broadside. There is a tendency for weak club and semi-skilled players to come unstuck in uncharted waters (unfamiliar openings). I shall stick with our semi-skilled player, else I'll start referring to Tal as Captain Cook!

As mentioned before, there is a pretty reasonable gun crew, but whilst the crew is still in need of further training they suddenly halt and turn to the navigators (positional play). The gun crew get sloppy (tactical ability starts to wane), and while this player can now discuss at great length the points of a double or isolated pawn, weak squares, etc., difficulty in nailing down small frigates (rabbits with teeth) remains.

Train the gun crew first, for without them you're *harmless*. Having reached a high standard of tactical ability, don't think it will always remain in peak condition. Keep your powder dry!

Fact

During the Napoleonic Wars the British and French fleets clashed many times. The French strategy was to aim at the ship's rigging, thus cutting down the manoeuvrability of the British ships (positional play).

The British trained their guns on the French gun crews and personnel (tactical play).

During the period 1793–1815 the French captured or sunk 17 British ships. The British, on the other hand, sunk or captured 229 French ships.*

You can't argue with mathematics like that . . . go for the throat!

Tactics and Combinations: Test Positions

The following positions (Diagrams 1–36) should illustrate and elaborate on many of the themes we have discussed already. They vary from the fairly easy to the extremely difficult but are not arranged in any particular order. Most of the solutions are very "clean" with one clear-cut answer to be found.

We suggest that you set each position up on your board and make a serious attempt to discover a definite best move or forcing line of play. If, after a few minutes, you are completely stuck, then look up the solution and you may discover some of the amazing possibilities which can lurk beneath the surface of a position. These test positions are the real "meat" of the lessons, in that it is very easy to learn nothing by breezing through a whole work of well-annotated examples, but it is a psychological law that greater attempts to achieve an object will be made if obstacles are put in the way. Also, chess is a game and solving these positions should be fun.

As a postscript, it is amusing that Bill Hartston once wrote a glowing review of a well-known book on tactics with the one criticism that he felt that tactical ability was conditioned mainly by experience and wondered if didactic works on the subject served any use at all!

Perhaps he was right, in which case we hope the reader enjoys solving these and accepts anything learned on the way as a bonus.

* James Henderson, *The Frigates*, Adlard-Coles Ltd.

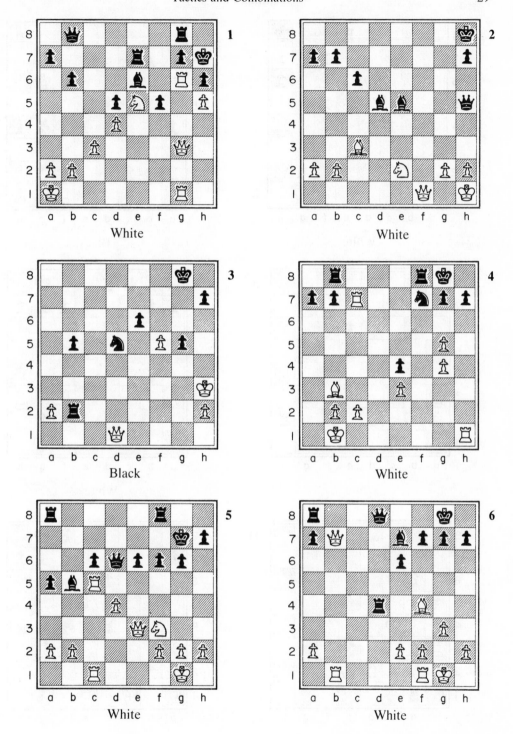

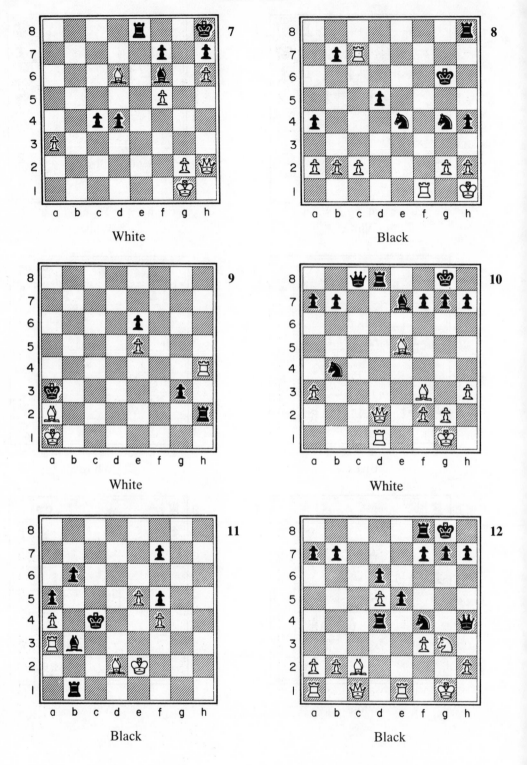

White   Black

White   White

Black   Black

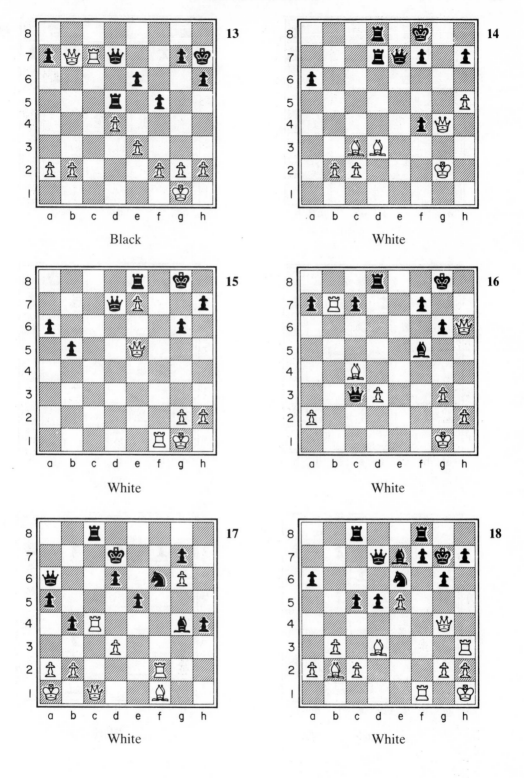

13

Black

14

White

15

White

16

White

17

White

18

White

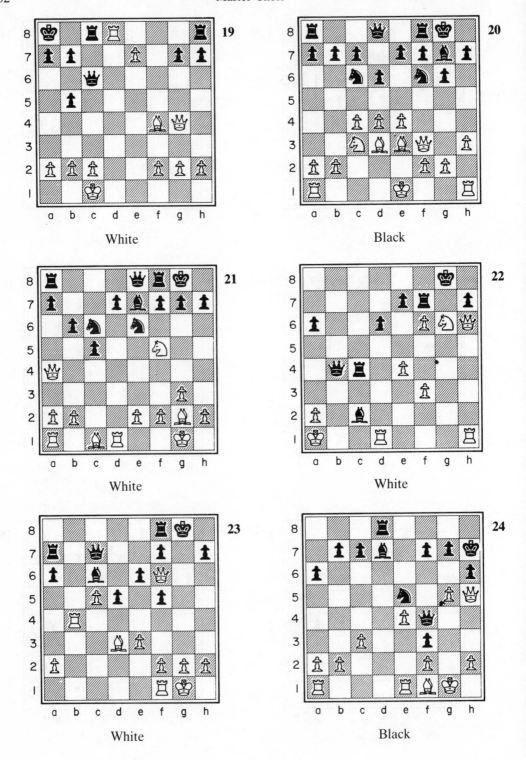

19   White

20   Black

21   White

22   White

23   White

24   Black

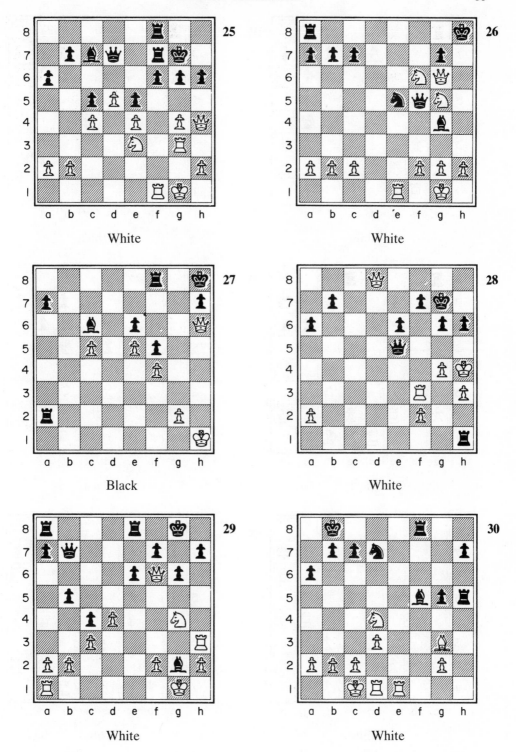

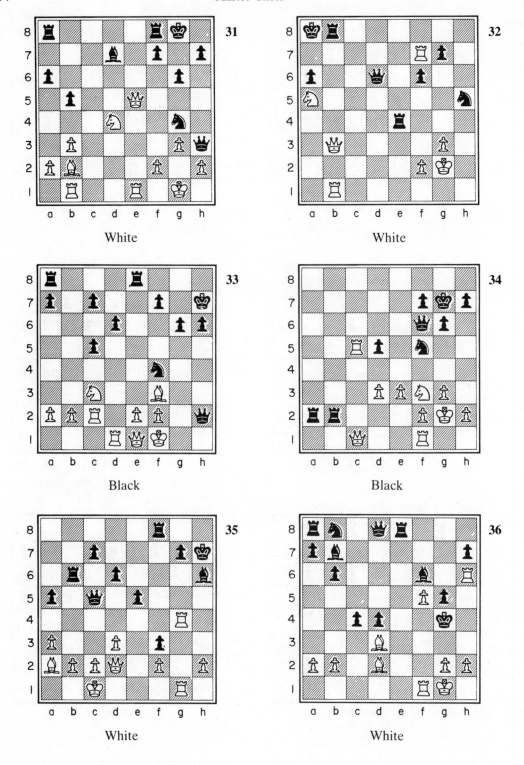

31

White

32

White

33

Black

34

Black

35

White

36

White

Lessons 5–8

HOW TO ANALYSE A POSITION

DANNY KOPEC, I.M.

LESSON 5. AN INTRODUCTION TO POSITIONAL ANALYSIS

More than 10 years of experience in master play and the teaching of private students or classes with players below master strength has convinced me that there are essentially three areas where nearly all such players prove deficient. These three areas, comprising Lessons 6, 7 and 8 are:

1. The basic question, "What is my opponent threatening?" is not answered.
2. The essential logic, features, and goals of a position are not deciphered.
3. The ability to draw on previous experiences (i.e. patterns), both good and bad, and to formulate the appropriate plan for a position, is lacking.

Of course, the degree of deficiency in each of these areas where errors in approach occur may vary over a large range. For example, when we say "not considering the threat or threats in a position", this may in some cases refer to a move which is an outright blunder because the opponent's *immediate* (1-move) threat has been overlooked. At the other extreme, the threat may be a *forcing sequence* of moves which leads to a win by acquisition of material, checkmate, or deterioration of position. The root of the problem in such instances is not an inability to analyse deeply enough, but an ignorance of the necessities or tactics in a position (or a certain laziness) which results in a key move, a "sting at the end of the tail", a certain check, pin, fork or double attack, being missed. Experience has

convinced me that even strong players, particularly those in the 1800–2000 (BCF 150–175) range, are often prone to such errors in missing the best move at the end of a 4- or 5-move sequence. Here I am not referring to positions which are essentially very intricate by nature (though any "simple-looking" chess position may have deep underlying complexities), but positions which are relatively straightforward, analysable, and therefore have small *branching factors*. For our purposes, the branching factor is the number of "plausible" moves at each level in the "tree" (Fig. 1) of legal moves from a given position. Thus, for example, from the starting position in chess White has 20 legal moves, but for practical purposes only 5 or 6 (e4, d4, c4, Nf3, b3 and possibly g3) need to be considered as likely to lead to any edge for White. Here the branching factor is 6 and in general middle-game positions the branching factor seems to average 7.

The ability to break down a position into its *essential features*, both tactical (such as pins, forks, double attacks, masked attacks, checks, and overloads, etc.) and positional (such as open or half-open files, pawn groups, and pawn weaknesses), is necessary to facilitate the process of selecting plausible moves.

With the above information, extractable from any position, we can now address the problem of deciding on a *plan* for a given position. The famous old saying cannot be over-emphasized:

> "It is better to play with a plan, albeit a bad one, than to play without a plan at all."

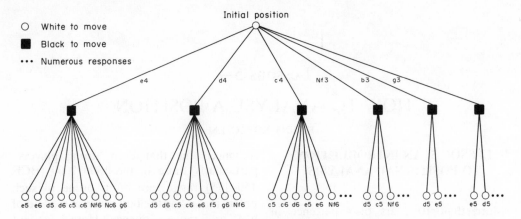

Fig. 1. Sample game tree of plausible moves from initial
position. Note that as White's first move takes less of
the centre, Black obtains more choices with which to
respond.

You should always consider the type of goal
position you're after.

The three main flaws outlined on p. 35
will be emphasized and supported with
examples, but some other problems such as
illogical play in the opening, impractical
play, and the use of published analysis will
also be considered.

As an example, let us ask:

"Why did White lose the following
game?"

Game 1

(Polish Opening) 1 b4 e5 2 Bb2 d6 3 c4 Nf6 4
e3 Be7 5 Nf3 0–0 6 Be2 Bf5 7 0–0 h6 8 d4 e4 9
Nfd2 c6 10 Nc3 d5 11 cxd5 cxd5 12 b5 Nbd7
13 a4 Re8 14 Qb3 Nf8 15 f3 exf3 16 Nxf3 Bd6
17 Ne5 Be6 18 Bf3 Bxe5 19 dxe5 d4 20 Qa3
dxc3 21 Bxc3 Ng4 White resigns.

Now we shall decipher the main events in
this "short play" which led to White's early
resignation. It is short enough to look at on
a move-by-move basis.

1 b4

While this move is certainly playable
and probably not bad, it would be hard
to argue that it is White's best or even
that it offers a first move initiative.

1 ... e5

Black takes as much of the centre as he
can get. The choice of e-pawn or d-
pawn is academic, though the e-pawn
allows early castling.

2 Bb2

White develops and attacks the e-pawn.

2 ... d6

Black makes it clear that he wants to
keep his e-pawn and has no intention of
attempting to refute White's opening.
When you get down to it, what other
sound moves were there? 2 ... Nc6?
invites 3 b5 Nd4 4 e3 and White wins a
pawn; 2 ... Bd6 breaks principles;
2 ... Qe7 is eccentric; only 2 ... f6!?
with the intention of blocking White's
queen's bishop with a pawn wall is a
profound alternative.

3 c4

This move fits White's hypermodern
start.

3 ... Nf6

Black develops modestly. More ambitious alternatives here were 3 ... f5
and 3 ... a5. The latter seems wrong in
principle: why open up the wing where

your opponent has more space unless you can prove it weak?

4 e3

White continues his non-committal approach. Also possible in the same vein were 4 g3, d3 or Nc3.

4 ... Be7

This and the next few moves require no comment.

5 Nf3 0–0 6 Be2 Bf5

Here Black continues to fight for as much of the centre as possible without making over-committal pawn moves. Again 6 ... Nc6 too simply invites 7 b5 and after 7 ... Nbd7 the knight would have no particular future.

7 0–0 h6

Not an important move, though one which is often useful in providing a haven for the queen's bishop on h7 if necessary. 7 ... e4?! 8 Nd4 Bg6 would not be effective here since White can follow with 9 d3, f3 or f4.

8 d4?!

Arguably, the game's first mistake. More cautious and logical was 8 d3, contending the e4 square. Now Black is able to set up a good reversed French formation with no particular problems.

8 ... e4 9 Nfd2 c6!

Discouraging 10 d5 and preparing to support his e-pawn with that move himself.

10 Nc3 d5

Black is still anxious to prevent d5 by White. However, on the more patient 10 ... Re8 11 b5 c5 (11 ... cxb5 12 Nxb5! with White better) 12 f3!? would keep up the tension.

11 cxd5?

A clear error. White releases the tension. Normal and correct was 11 b5

when cxb5 12 Nxd5 (also 12 Nxb5! but not 12 cxd5? b4 wins a pawn) 12 ... Nxd5 13 cxd5 Qxd5 14 a4! would leave White with interesting counter-chances for a pawn.

11 ... cxd5 12 b5

This move is correctly motivated (queen-side counterplay), but 12 Qb3 was more to the point (faster) as it prevents 12 ... Nbd7.

12 ... Nbd7 13 a4?!

Again 13 Qb3 and then on 13 ... Be6 14 f3! Instead White switches from plan to plan. It seems he intends 14 Ba3, trading off his bad bishop.

13 ... Re8 14 Qb3!?

Here 14 Ba3 was consistent, though the text is not bad.

14 ... Nf8 15 f3!

White decides to keep up the pressure on Black's d-pawn, but then what was the point of 12 b5 and 13 a4?

15 ... exf3

No choice.

16 Nxf3?

But what's this? 16 Bxf3 forcing 16 ... Be6 was essential. Black is now able to achieve two goals with his next move.

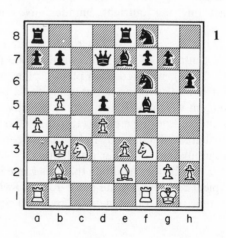

16 ... Bd6!

These are:

(1) The White e pawn is exposed to frontal attack.

(2) The Black king's bishop obtains the b8–h2 diagonal. The d-pawn is, of course, still defended indirectly.

17 Ne5!?

Under pressure, White makes a stab for counterplay. Certainly 17 Nd1 was distasteful.

17 ... Be6

Not 17 ... Bxe5?? 18 dxe5 Rxe5 19 Nd1 and wins. The calm retreat opens a threat on the knight on e5.

18 Bf3??

Having been under some pressure for the past few moves, White blunders horribly (not analysing the threat or the simplest move — or has he just forgotten it?). On the necessary retreats 18 Nf3 or 18 Nd3 Black has many pleasant continuations, e.g. 18 Nf3 Ne4, 18 ... Ng4, 18 ... N8h7, 18 ... Ng6 or 18 ... Bg4, or on 18 Nd3 N8h7 looks best, though 18 ... Qc7!? and 18 ... Ne4 deserve attention too. The rest needs no explanation.

18 ... Bxe5 19 dxe5 d4 20 Qa3 dxc3 21 Bxc3 Ng4 White resigns.

So why did White lose so quickly? Was it just one big outright blunder? No, not exactly.

First, he unnecessarily ceded ground in the centre (8 d4); then he wasted time (12 b5, 13 a4), wavered from plan to plan, and left himself with no counterplay for a permanent weakness (pawn on e3). Finally, he blundered, losing a piece (18 Bf3??). So his final great blunder may in fact have been an accumulation of earlier problems.

It may be worth adding that this game is a typical 2nd round game in a 5-round, Swiss-system open tournament (Cape Cod $500

Open, 1976) where the top-rated player (this writer, 2346 at the time) meets one of the lowest players (James Quirk, 1763). This game was intended to show the gradual decline of the weaker player in a strategically based game. In a tactically based game the loser's demise can, by contrast, be quite abrupt and easy to pinpoint.

LESSON 6. WHAT ARE THE THREATS IN THE POSITION?

Consider the following position from the 1981 Glasgow Herald Open in the game Kleboe (1835)–Weeden (1950) after 16 ... Qc5.

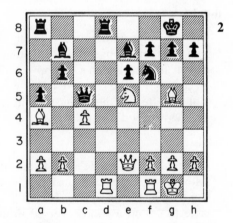

It is important to develop the habit of considering automatically all forced capture sequences *with every move*. Had White done so he would have continued 17 Bxf6 Bxf6 18 Nd7 with a big plus, i.e. 18 ... Qg5? 19 f4 Qg6 20 Bc2 Qh6 21 Nxb6 and White wins a pawn, since if 21 ... Bd4+ 22 Rxd4. You might say that this is five full moves from the starting position, but after 18 ... Qg5? they were all forced. One try for Black would be 18 ... Qb4 (attacking the bishop and b-pawn), but then simply 19 b3 (threatening 20 Bb5 and even better than 19 Nxf6+) would leave him in great difficulties. Best would therefore be 18 ... Qc7.

Instead play continued: 17 Rfe1 Rac8 18 Nxf7(!??) (18 Bb5 would leave White clearly better) White sacrifices his best posted piece for no clear compensation. Black should have accepted and seen what White had in mind after 18 ... Kxf7 19 Qxe6+ Kf8. 18 ... Rxd1 19 Bxd1 (the move Weeden missed (!?) but had he seen 19 ... Qc6! threatening mate and guarding e6, he would have foiled White's ploy) 19 ... Kxf7? 20 Qxe6+ Kf8 21 Bh5 resigns.

Example 2

In the following position from Samuelian (2268)–Burnham (1920) from the New Hampshire Open (USA, 1981) after 23 moves of play White decides to end the game by direct tactical means, aiming for a king-side attack by 24 Qh4?!. Correct was 24 a5 when Black's a-pawn was doomed while White could keep his, along with the better position.

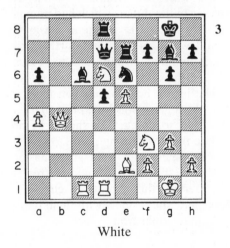

White

Instead the game went: 24 Qh4 Bxa4 25 Rxd5 Bc6 26 Nf5? (Here 26 Rxc6 Qxc6 27 Qxe7 Qxd5 28 Qxf7+ Kh8 29 Bc4! Qd1+ 30 Kg2 would appear to win for White; if the knight on e6 moves, then 31 Qg8+! mates, but 30 ... Rf8 turns the tables. A better winning attempt is 29 Ng5!) 26 ... Bxd5 27 Nxe7+ Kh8 (better was Kf8) 28 Rd1 Qb7 29 Bxa6? (29 Ng5 wins simply, with threats on

the rook on d8 and pinned bishop on d5 in addition to the mates on h7 and f7) Qxa6 30 Rxd5 Rxd5 31 Nxd5 Bxe5! This leaves the game level, (e.g. 32 Nxe5 Qa1+ recovers the piece) but not before some final fireworks 32 Qe7 Qd6 33 Qxf7 Qxd5 34 Ng5 Qd1+ 35 Kg2 Nf4+! 36 gxf4 Qg4+ 37 Kf1 Qd1+ 38 Kg2 Qg4+ 39 Kf1 Qd1+ 40 Kg2 Draw.

Now consider the following game played at the 1980 Malta Olympiad between two very sharp players, Ghinda (Romania) and Sax (Hungary).

Game 2

(**Sicilian Defence**) **1 e4 c5 2 Nf3 d6 3 d4 cxd4 4 Nxd4 Nf6 5 Nc3 g6 6 Bg5 Bg7 7 Bb5+ Bd7 8 Qe2 Nc6 9 0–0–0 Rc8 10 Bxc6 bxc6 11 f4 0–0 12 e5 dxe5 13 fxe5 Nd5 14 Nxd5 cxd5 15 e6 fxe6 16 Nxe6 Qb6 17 Nxg7 Rf2 18 Qd3 Kxg7 19 Rd2 Bf5 20 Be3 Bxd3 21 Bxf2 Qf6 White resigns**.

After a "first viewing" the reader should be convinced that something went terribly wrong in the midst of White's aggressive intentions, initiated by 12 e5. You should also be suspicious of White's crudely simple opening play and Black's almost disdainful responses to it. An alternative requiring consideration was 8 ... Bxb5 when neither 9 Qxb5+ Qd7 nor 9 Ndxb5 Nbd7 offers White much. At 9 ... Rc8 Black's position was already critical, e.g. if 9 ... Nxd4 10 Rxd4 Bxb5 11 Nxb5 a6 12 e5! (12 Nxd6+ exd6 13 e5! also wins) axb5 13 exf6 is crushing, and 10 Bxc6 followed by 11 e5 was threatened. However, 11 f4 proved to be over ambitious.

Another serious alternative was 11 e5. Then a sample continuation could go: 11 ... dxe5 12 Qxe5 0–0

(see following diagrams)

13 Rhe1 Nd5 14 Nxd5!?? (14 Bxe7? Bxe5 15 Bxd8 Bxd4 wins a piece for Black) Bxe5 15 Nxe7+ (or 15 Bxe7 Bxd4 16 Bxd8 cxd5 −+) Kh8 (15 ... Kg7 16 Nef5+ gxf5 17 Bxd8

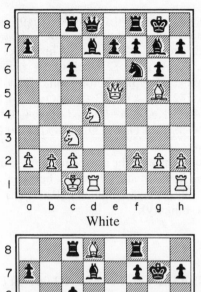

White

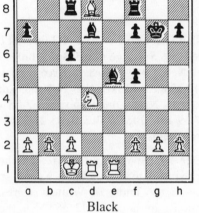

Black

wins, or on 15 Bxe7 Qb6! etc., with Black better. Hence after 12 ... 0–0 we must again reconsider White's alternatives, for 13 ... Nd5 is definitely threatened. It is clear that the White queen must move; the question is "Where to?" 13 Qc5 is most enterprising, though 13 Qg3 and 13 Qe3 are both probably sounder. The point of all this analysis is that only now can we conclude:

1. 11 e5 was a serious alternative for White.
2. Then, however, after 11 ... dxe5 12 Qxe5 0–0 Black would threaten Nd5 taking over the initiative.

As play went, 12 e5 was sharpest but premature. Deserving attention instead was 12 Nf3. 13 ... Nd5 could merit "!!" if Sax had seen this move and its ramifications early enough. Suddenly the stroke 16 ... Qb6! revealed Black's ominous designs. The full depth of his tactical conception blossomed with 18 ... Kxg7!. Ghinda has no answer to the threats which had mounted on c2 after 19 ... Bf5 as on 21 Bxb6 Rxc2+ would win a piece. With further material losses imminent, White had to resign after 21 ... Qf6.

The lesson here is that you must always ask why a game was lost, particularly if it is short. In so doing, you should be able to isolate the key turning points.

Sometimes even solid grandmasters are prone to this most common error in not considering the threat(s), checks, pins, forks, etc., but usually with them they occur in a more sophisticated form.

(diagram) 17 ... Bxd4 18 Rxd4 either R/xd8 19 Red1 which should win) 16 Nxg6+ hxg6 Bxd8 and wins as in the footnote. But how many readers missed 17 ... Bf4+? This is a typical "A-player" blunder, missing that key intermezzo (in between) move, check, or other such twist which completely alters the result. Instead, in the main line above White may try 16 Rxe5 (threatening 17 Bf6 mate) but then simply 17 ... f6 would again leave us unconvinced about the soundness of White's combination, i.e. 18 Ndxc6 Qe8 (18 ... Bxc6? 19 Rxd8 Rcxd8 20 Nxc6 Rd6 and it's only unclear; 18 ... Qc7!?) 19 Nxc8 fxe5 20 Nd6 Qe6 21 Nd8 Qg4 and Black takes over.

So you might quite justifiably ask, why get carried away in all this generosity (14 Nxd5!??) when you could play a sane move like 14 Qg3? Well then 14 ... Nxc3 would have to be considered, but on 15 Qxc3 c5!

Game 3

The diagrammed position was reached after the following moves in Korchnoi–Tarjan (Lone Pine 1981) Nimzo–Indian (via Queen's Indian) Defence.

1 d4 Nf6 2 c4 e6 3 Nf3 b6 4 Nc3 Bb7 5 Bf4 Bb4 6 Qb3 a5 7 e3 d6 8 Be2 Ne4 9 0–0 Bxc3 10 bxc3.

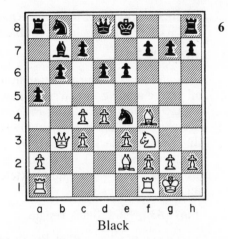

Black

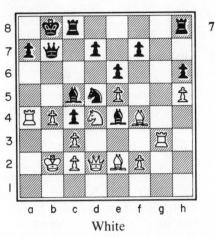

White

Black could have obtained quite a solid game with 10 ... 0–0 or 10 ... Nd7. Instead he played 10 ... g5?! leading to 11 Bxg5 Nxg5 12 Qb5+ Nd7 13 Qxg5 Qxg5 14 Nxg5. It is unlikely that a grandmaster of Tarjan's calibre simply overlooked 11 Bxg5, but more than likely that after the continuation 14 ... Bxg2 15 Kxg2 Rg8 16 f4 h6 17 h4 f6 he missed 18 Bg4, winning a pawn (since on 18 ... Nf8 19 Nxe6! Rxg4+ 20 Kh3) and the game. For the record this is how Korchnoi did it: 18 ... Ke7 19 Bxe6 Rg7 20 Bxd7 Kxd7 21 e4 (Korchnoi insists on connected d-pawns) c1 ... c5 22 e5 dxe5 23 dxe5 fxe5 24 Rad1+ Kc7 25 Kh3 (finally the knight must be taken) 25 ... hxg5 26 fxg5 e4 27 Rde1 Rd8 28 Rxe4 Rd3+ 29 Kg4 Rxc3 30 h5 resigns.

Example 3

As a final example for this lesson on analysing threats, see what you think of the following position which arose after 27 tense moves of play in the first game of my two-game play-off match with Roddy McKay for the 1980 Scottish Championship.

(see following diagram)

Earlier in the game I had been sure that I stood better due to superior central control (pawn on e5 holding Black's d-, e- and f-pawns) and control of the open g-file and half-open a-file. However, after Black's last

move, 27 ... Bf8–c5), the position suddenly became rich with complications. The apparently precarious position of the White king means that a sacrifice on b4 had to be considered on Black's last move, i.e. 27 ... Nxb4, but fortunately after 28 Rxb4 Bxb4 29 cxb4, White's rook on g3 guards against the fork on c3. Black does threaten 28 ... Bxd4 29 Qxd4 (29 cxd4 c3+ wins) 29 ... Nxf4 simply winning a piece. To cope with this, if White tries to move either knight or queen's bishop to a safe square such as 28 Be3? or 28 Nf3?, then the rook's defence of c3 is interfered with and a combination on b4 becomes possible. On any 28th move by the White king (or on 28 Qc1) 28 ... Bxd4 29 cxd4 c3 would win for Black.

So what should White play? I was sure my position could not have suddenly become lost from just that one move, 27 ... Bc5, finally completing Black's development. I even considered 28 Nb3!? with the idea that on 28 ... cxb3 29 Ba6 Qc6 30 b5! leaving Black's queen, bishop, and rook *en prise*, must win, e.g. 30 ... Qb6 31 Rxe4 Qa5 32 cxb3 Qa3+ 33 Kc2 Qa2+ 34 Kd3!. But I hesitated, reluctant to embark on great complications from what had been a "pure" plus; and indeed after 28 Nb3!!? Bxf2 29 Na5 Qb5 30 Bxc4 Rxc4 31 Qxf2 the position would become even more unclear, e.g. 31 ... Qxa4 32 Nxc4 Nxf4 33 Nd6! and White still has compensation for his piece deficit.

Instead, in mutual time pressure I played 28 Bxh6??! and the continuation was:

28 ... Bxd4 29 Bg7

I had simply forgotten that on 29 Qxd4 Nb6 allows the black queen to protect his bishop while White's rook and bishop are left hanging.

29 ... Bxf2

Here post-mortem analysis showed that 29 ... Nxb4! 30 Kc1 Nd3+ wins; in horrendous time pressure McKay now produced a series of blunders which ultimately cost him the championship:

30 Rh3 Nb6?

Correct was 30 ... Bg2 with the idea 31 ... Be3 or 31 ... a5.

31 Ra5 Rhg8 32 h6

Now White has play for his piece.

32 ... Bh7? 33 Rf3?! (33 Bf3 wins a piece immediately) **33 ... Bh4 34 Rxf7 Bd8 35 Bf3 Qc7 36 Bf8 Bg6 37 Bd6 Bxf7 38 Qd4?!**

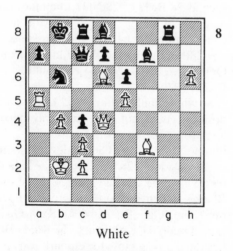

White

Here I missed a last chance to win quickly by 38 h7 Rh8 39 Qd4 (with the idea 40 Qxb6+) 39 ... Qxd6 40 exd6 Rxh7 41 Qe4 which is decisive.

38 ... Qxd6 39 exd6 Bg6 40 Qd1 Bh7 41 Qd4

The sealed move after some "hectic"

play, but not 41 Qa1? for 41 ... Rg3 42 Rxa7 Rxf3 43 Qa6 would win for Black!

41 ... Rf8 42 Bg2?!

After an hour's adjournment analysis I still played a move I knew to be flawed — that is McKay could have got the edge with 42 ... e5! in that on 43 Qxe5 Rf2 wins for Black, or 43 Rxe5 Bf6 wins, and on 43 Qe3 he could follow with 43 ... e4. Instead, McKay blunders unbelievably:

42 ... Bf6?? 43 Qxb6+ Black resigns.

Not a game of which either Roddy or I could be proud, but one which is instructive and entertaining, particularly for its blunders!

LESSON 7. WHAT ARE THE ESSENTIAL FEATURES OF A POSITION?

Before you can consider what the correct move might be in a position, you need to identify its key components. These assessments should be on a tactical and structural basis. This includes interactions of opposing forces in terms of pins, forks, double attacks, checks, etc., as covered in the lessons on Tactics and Combinations by Geoff Chandler and the overall structural foundations of a position such as doubled pawns, open and half-open files, etc., as covered in the lessons on How to Formulate a Plan by Chris Morrison. Having performed these assessments methodically, it is then possible to consider what the correct (best) move(s) in a position might be.

Example 4

The diagrammed position is now famous for the careful scrutiny to which it has been subjected by the psychologist and chess master Adrian de Groot (1965) and Newell and Simon (1972):

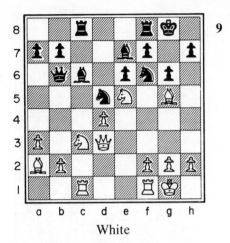

White

De Groot's opening comments:

"Taken from a game between A.D. de Groot–C. Scholtens, April 10, 1936. White is on move . . . This position mainly presents problems of a tactical nature. Through his last move (... Qb6) Black has created a "hanging position" for his bishop on e7; it is defended only by the exchangeable knight on d5 so that the black knight on f6 is somewhat tied down. There are all sorts of exchange possibilities in the centre and the question is whether or not it is possible for White to make some profitable use of the tactical weaknesses in Black's position. If no such possibility should exist, White could best strengthen his position with some calm move.

From a thorough analysis, however, it appears that White is in a position to get the better of it; there is even a forced win. The winning move is 1 Bxd5 . . ." (de Groot, 1965, section 26).

Newell and Simon devote some 40 intensive pages to the study of the behaviour of a single subject (S2), an average, active college club player of about 1600 strength, for the analysis of this position. This is not the place to go into Newell and Simon's research in detail, but we can briefly summarize the behaviour of S2. He analyses the position for 17 minutes, consisting of some 25 "episodes" which have been split into 7

"scenes". These scenes roughly consist of (with cumulative times given):

Scene 1 (0 sec). Orientation, material examination, Black's threats.

Scene 2 (80 sec). Examines 1 Bxd5 and 1 Qf3, considering Black's possible counter-attacks.

Scene 3 (300 sec). Considers other moves such as 1 Nxc6, 1 Nxf7, 1 Nxg6, 1 Rc2, and king-side pawn pushes, finding nothing.

Scene 4 (385 sec). Re-examines 1 Bxd5; checks Black's counter-attack 1 ... Qxb2, finds White wins a piece for pawn or two. Sees that 1 ... Nxd5 defends Black on e7 and finds that 1 ... Bxd5 2 Nxd5 Nxd5 also leaves the bishop on e7 defended.

Scene 5 (540 sec). Starts to look at king-side attacking ideas such as 1 Bh6 and 1 Ne4 or 1 Ne4, but fears 1 Ne4 Qxb2 with the bishop on a2 hanging. Concludes that 1 Bxd5 should be the initial move.

Scene 6 (735 sec). Re-evaluates 1 Bxd5. Finds that 1 ... Bxd5 can be met by 2 Na4 leading to advantage for White; thus examines 1 ... exd5 and also concludes that isolated pawn gives White edge. Finds that 1 ... Nxd5 2 Nxd5 also loses for Black. Concludes 1 ... exd5 necessary.

Scene 7 (980 sec). Decides that best move is 1 Bxd5.

It is fairly clear from the above "scenario" that while the subject ultimately chooses the correct move, his reasons for doing so are not convincing. There are several important details missing in his analysis and throughout he "appears to be ignorant of several of the essential features of the position" (Newell and Simon).

All humans are known to carry out a process of "progressive deepening" (de Groot, 1965) in their analysis of a position. That is, we tend to deepen the extent of our analysis of a position in successive stages.

This process, which entails returning to previously analysed moves, rehashing, re-checking, and extending variations from them, is not by any means an efficient one, but due to the limitations of our memories (in contrast to computers) we find this is the best way to "take account" of what we have considered.

A fact which is in further contradiction with popular beliefs is that grandmasters' unique talent does not lie in the ability to calculate all the possibilities down the tree of variations. Instead, they typically con-sider some 30–50 nodes (future board pos-itions) from a given one, with a maximum of 100 or so. They are particularly adept in looking at a position and extracting the essential features quickly. It is as if they approach the witty remark attributed to Reti when asked how many moves he looked ahead from a given position: "Only one move, the best one", he replied.

In his analysis of the diagrammed position the subject misses one important, recurring theme: it is that White will have a fork on d7 (Nd7) winning the exchange in a number of variations.

For example, in the line 1 Bxd5 Bxd5 2 Nxd5 Nxd5 he sees that the black on e7 is defended, but never mentions that after 3 Bxe7 Nxe7 4 Nd7, White wins the exchange (though it's essential for White to see further that 4 ... Rxc1 5 Rxc1 Qxb2 6 Rb1 still wins). Later the subject also comes to the correct conclusion that 1 ... Bxd5 loses, but for the wrong reason. He mentions 2 Na4 instead of the above. Hence, also for the wrong reasons, he is able to conclude that 1 ... exd5 is essential. He never quite hits upon the strength of 2 Qf3! (though considers it as White's first move). Now Black must play 2 ... Qd8 (if 2 ... Kg7 3 Ng4! threatening the knight on f6) and 3 Bh6+ wins since 3 ... Nxg4 4 Bxe7 Rfe8 (4 ... Nxh2? 5 Bxf8+ (*CHECK*)) 5 Bc5 is decisive. Now the strong move which lesser players would typically miss is 3 Rce1. This threatens 4 Ng4 again, i.e. 4 ... Nxg4 5 Bxe7 wins. Once again 4 ... Kg7 is of no help so

the only moves left to consider are those which might meet the threat(s):

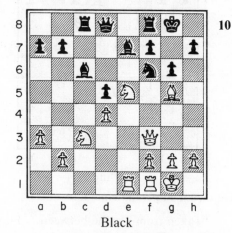

Black

(A)   3 ... Re8 allows White to win a pawn after 4 Nxc6 Rxc6 (4 ... bxc6 5 Rxe7 and 6 Bxf6+−) 5 Bxf6 Bxf6 (5 ... Rxf6 6 Qxd5) 6 Rxe8+ Qxe8 7 Qxd5.

(B)   3 ... Ne4 (a clarifying move which is essential to consider) 4 Bxe7 Qxe7 5 Nxc6 bxc6 (5 ... Rxc6 6 Nxd5) 6 Nxe4 and White wins a solid pawn.

(C)   3 ... h5 4 Nxc6 Rxc6 (again 4 ... bxc6 5 Rxe7) 5 Rxe7! and herein lies the point — on 3 Rfe1 which looked more normal, Black could now play 5 ... Qxe7 6 Nxd5 Rxc1+ and win. With 3 Rfe1 if White now resorted to 5 Bxf6 Bxf6 6 Nxd5 Rxc1 (not 6 ... Bxd4 7 Rxc6 and 8 Ne7+) 7 Rxc1 Bxd4, he should have considered very seriously the consequences of 8 Rc8!?? , because after 8 ... Qxc8 9 Ne7+ Kg7 10 Nxc8 Rxc8 it's not at all clear. Probably White's best would therefore be 8 Rc7.

(D)   3 ... Rc7; with the above analysis it is now easy to find that 4 Nxc6 Rxc6 (or 4 ... bxc6) 5 Rxe7 and 6 Nxd5 wins.

The reader should note that 1 Bxd5! was not the standard move in this sort of position, giving up the two bishops, but because of Black's forced recapture, 1 ... exd5, leaving a bad light-squared for Black (and White's threats to follow) it was best. This example has been covered in great detail to illustrate just what is meant by "considering the threat(s)" (such as forkability on d7, pins on f6, intermezzo checks) and the "essential features" (such as bad bishops, loose pieces, and back rank counter-threats) in a position.

Example 5

The following position occurred in the 1978 Golden Knights (US Correspondence Championship) Finals between Burnham (White) and Bailey (Black).

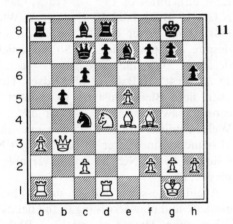

Burnham gives 20 ... Rxa3 a "?" but what could Black play? The main threats are (A) 21 Nxb5, (B) 21 Nf5 and (C) 21 Qg3. Most of White's dangerous threats stem from the cramping effect of the pawn on e5. That is, Black's d-pawn is kept backward on d7 which means the queen's bishop is locked, keeping the rooks disconnected and f5 is accessible to White's pieces.

Therefore 20 ... Nxe5 is essential to consider. Then White's tries are:

(A)　21 Nxb5 Qb8 22 Qg3 Qxb5 23 Bxe5 f6 (23 ... Bf8 24 Bd6!) 24 Rd6 and Black's troubles are not over.

(B)　21 Nf5 Bf6?! 22 Nd6 Nc4 is unclear, but 22 Rd6! is crushing; best is 21 ... d6 22 Nxe7+ (22 Bxe5 Bxf5) Qxe7 23 Bxe5 Qxe5 24 Bxc6 which doesn't offer White anything.

(C)　21 Qg3 d6! (21 ... Bf6?! 22 Nxb5 [not 22 Nf5 d5!] followed by Nd6) 22 Bxe5 dxe5 23 Nxc6 Rxd1+ 24 Rxd1 Rxa3 25 Nxe7+ Qxe7 26 Qxe5! would win at least a pawn for White; or on 24 ... Bb7 25 Nxe7+ Qxe7 26 Bxb7 Qxb7 27 Qxe5 would win a pawn since 27 ... Rxa3 28 Rd8+ Kh7 29 Qf5+ g6 30 Qf6 is decisive. However, Black does have a key alternative in this line in 24 ... Ra4 which leaves the position in the balance.

I must apologize here to readers for all these long variations. It is not my intention to overwhelm you, but to indicate the inherent intricacies in any position where there are long capture sequences, threats, and counter-threats, and the necessity to analyse them thoroughly. In the present game the fact that it was a correspondence game meant that Black should have given 20 ... Nxe5 sufficient attention. The game continued:

21 Rxa3 Bxa3 22 Qg3 (White's threats are now decisive) Qa7 23 Bxh6! Bf8 24 Bxg7 Qa3 25 Qg5 when Black should resign in view of 25 ... Bxg7 26 Nf5 Qf8 27 Nh6+ Kh8 28 Qf5 Qg8 29 Nxf7+ Qxf7 30 Qh7 mate.

Example 6

The following position occurred in the game Orr–Moultrie from the second round of the 1981 Scottish Championship.
Black is the exchange up and has a sound, solid position. White has weakened his kingside with the advances g4, g5, and h4 in an attempt to obtain counterplay there. Plausible moves are (1) 33 ... Qh3, exchanging off queens; (2) 33 ... Nd3, forking White's

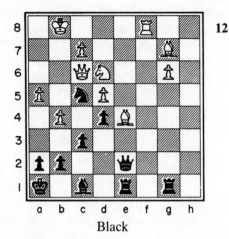

Black   Black

rook and bishop; (3) 33 ... Nxd5, reducing material, though also relinquishing Black's best posted piece, while White can re-capture with the knight with much pressure on f6; (4) 33 ... Be7, pressing g5 and de-fending f6; (5) 33 ... fxg5, with the intention that on 34 hxg5 Nh3+ wins the g-pawn. All these moves are logical in one way or another, though their effectiveness can only be determined by considering concrete vari-ations.

Instead, due to the usual problem of time pressure, Black's game dissipated with the illogical 33 ... Qb5? and the game con-cluded: 34 Bc4 Qe8 35 gxf6 gxf6 36 Nf5 Rbc8 37 Kh2 Bc5? 38 Qxf4! Bd4 39 Qh6 Qg6 40 Qxg6 hxg6 41 Nxd4 exd4 42 Rd1 and Black resigned. Of course time pressure never helps!

Example 7

The diagrammed position arose after 13 Ne4 in the game Kopec vs. the late Ian Wells, Manchester, 1981.

There is really nothing wrong with Black's position except for the slightly cramping effect of the white e-pawn which he may feel. Since he just played 12 ... Rb8 (to prevent Nd2–b3) I expected 13 ... b5 followed by 14 ... a5, with a general queen-side expansion, or a rational move such as 13 ... Qc7, i.e. 14 Ng3 Rfc8.

Instead, without much thought, Wells took up the gauntlet and indulged in 13 ... Ncxe5?! when after 14 Nxe5 Nxe5 15 Bf4, he did not want to cope with the long-term difficulties of 15 ... f6 (15 ... Qa5 16 Nd2!) 16 Bxe5 fxe5 17 Qg4 when White must stand better due to the e4 outpost, despite his pawn deficit. So he quickly decided on the exchange sacrifice 15 ... Nxc4!? 16 Bxb8 Qxb8 17 dxc4. How-ever, here Black must try to connect his central pawns with 17 ... f6 or 17 ... e5. Wells' continuation 17 ... f5 was a position-al blunder, since after 18 Nd2 Bf6 19 Nf3 followed by 20 Ne5 he was never able to play ... e5.

Again the lesson is that you should always evaluate and play according to the needs of the position. Having played 12 ... Rb8, 13 ... Ncxe5 was an illogical move if only because it invited the unpleasant pin 15 Bf4. Black's further error was that having em-barked on this path, he did not consider sufficiently the pros and cons of the interest-ing exchange sacrifice 15 ... Nxc4.

Example 8

To close this lesson on "the essential features of a position" I give a further example from my two-game play-off match with Roddy McKay (March, 1981). The following critical position in the 2nd game arose after 19 Re1.

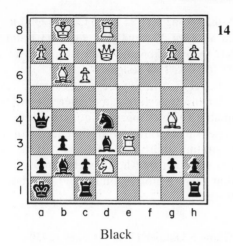

14

Black

White has recovered two pawns sacrificed in the opening with his rook on d6 and knight on e7 and it appears that Black's knight on e5 is in great peril. Could it really be trapped on an active square in the middle of the board!?

Already having more than an hour time advantage, I gave the position considerable thought. Any knight move would appear to lose at least a pawn, i.e. 19 ... Nc6, as would the counter-attack on White's nearly trapped knight on e7, 19 ... Qg5, i.e. 20 Bxe5 Qxe7 21 Bc4! (21 Bxg7+ Kxg7 22 Qe5+ Qf6 is not clear).

What to play then? I looked at 19 ... a6, but then simply 20 Bxe5 axb5 21 Qxb5 still looked much better for White. I even considered the counter-stroke 19 ... Nxf3+ with the idea that on 20 gxf3 Qc5+ either picks up the hanging rook on d6 or bishop on b5 (after 21 Qf2). But of course the bishop on g3 would defend that rook after 19 ... Nxf3+. The accumulation of all the above assessments, features and tactical motifs led me to find the perfect combination miniaturette in the position which went:

19 ... Nxf3+!! 20 gxf3 Qg5! Suddenly the "hanging" aspects of White's position are fully evident. There is no 21 Be5 (illegal!) and 21 Rxe6 fxe6 22 Qxe6 is impossible because the bishop on b5 hangs. Hence it is clear that Black must recover his lost knight, for the white knight is now truly trapped (d5

is covered) and with interest in that White's king-side pawn structure has been permanently damaged.

LESSON 8. INABILITY TO DRAW ON PREVIOUS EXPERIENCE TO FORM A PLAN

I have always contended that the games from which I have learned the most were losses or draws. These are the games which most painfully and vividly have impressed themselves on my chess memory, and therefore are the most valuable means to judge progress, or lack of it. But, admittedly, it is most upsetting when you lose or draw a game and there is no moral to be found, no lesson to be learned.

The following game was played about 12 years ago when I was then rated 2032 and faced Joshua Fluk (1650), a recent arrival from Israel, in the 1969–70 New York City Interscholastic H.S. Championships. Though we both had perfect scores 4/4, with the big rating difference I was considered to be the favourite. However, having observed a number of Fluk's games, I knew he was a good, natural player, not to be underestimated.

As it turned out, I was given a lesson never to be forgotten. On that occasion every move of Fluk's up to the decisive surprise stroke, 33 ... Nxg4, struck me as cold logic, and perfect, like those of a real champion:

Game 4 Kopec–Fluk, Nimzo–Indian Defence

1 d4 Nf6 2 c4 e6 3 Nc3 Bb4 4 e3 b6 5 Nf3 Bb7 6 Bd3 Ne4 7 Qc2 f5 8 0–0 Bxc3 9 bxc3 0–0

A standard opening with Black trying to maintain his grip on e4 and blockade the position as much as possible, particularly White's doubled c-pawns. White, on the other hand, should try to open the position as much as possible for his two bishops and central pawn mass.

10 a4

While this is not bad, with the goal of opening the position by Ba3, and c5, 10 Nd2 and 10 Ne1 are more common.

10 ... d6

I gave up on the idea of 11 Ba3 followed by c5 for it could not be enforced, and instead switched back to 11 Nd2.

11 Nd2 Nxd2 12 Bxd2 c5 13 d5

At the time I was already aware that in such positions it is essential for White to open the centre. 13 d5?! had this intention, but proved ineffective. Much better would have been 13 f4! (followed by e4) or 13 e4!?, though I rejected the latter blinded by my desire to win, e.g. 13 e4!? f4 14 e5 g6 15 Bxg6 hxg6 16 Qxg6+ =.

13 ... g6!

This showed Fluk's deep appreciation of the position in that the weakened black squares could not be exploited, e.g. 14 dxe6 Qf6 15 e4 f4 etc. My further efforts to open the position by 14 e4 and 15 g3 were thwarted by 14 ... f4 and 15 ... e5, closing the centre and leading to Fluk's quick re-organization utilizing his king-side spatial edge.

This was emphasized by 20 ... h5! followed by 23 ... Kf7 and 25 ... Rah8. I tried to hold back Black's king-side advances and even seemed to be making some progress on the queen-side with 30 axb6 but the stellar 30 ... a6 proved this too slow while Black proceeded with his incursions (31 ... Rh1 and 32 ... Qh3) capped by the decisive 33 ... Nxg4.

14 e4 f4 15 g3 e5 16 f3 Nd7 17 Qc1 g5 18 Rf2 Rf7 19 Be1 Qf8 20 g4 h5 21 h3 Rh7 22 Rh2

Nf6 23 Raa2 Kf7 24 Rag2 Qg7 25 Qb2 Rah8 26 a5 hxg4 27 hxg4 Rh3 28 Rxh3 Rxh3 29 Kf2 Qh6 30 axb6 a6 31 Bc2 Rh1 32 Ke2 Qh3 33 Rf2 Nxg4 34 resigns.

In relation to the previous example, consider the following game where White was unable to draw on previous experience to cope satisfactorily with the needs of the position and problems posed by Black. It is not so much that he plays bad moves, but that there is no resolution and direction in them.

Game 5 Dauber (1775)–Kopec (2430), 12th Manchester Congress, 1981, Round 5, Nimzo–Indian Defence

1 d4 Nf6 2 c4 e6 3 Nc3 Bb4 4 e3 b6 5 Nf3 Bb7 6 Bd2

There is nothing particularly wrong with this move except that it indicates White's unfamiliarity with the opening. The games of the "old masters" Nimzowitsch, Bogolyubov, and Alekhine demonstrated the move as inconsequential. More "theoretical" was 6 Bd3 as in the previous game.

6 ... 0–0 7 Be2 d6 8 0–0 Nbd7

Perhaps more accurate was 8 ... Bxc3, since the bishop has served its purpose.

9 Qb3 a5 10 Rad1 Bxc3 11 Bxc3 Qe7

With 10 Rad1 White indicated his intention to play d5. Black makes preparations for this and supports a possible ... e5 in any case. The more direct 11 ... Ne4 also deserves attention.

12 Nd2

White correctly plays to fight for the e4 square and from the previous game the reader should now know 13 f4 is in the air; hence Black's continuation; but what was the point of 10 Rad1? Here that rook on e1 would fit better.

12 ... e5 13 Qc2 Rfe8 14 Rfe1 h6

Black prepares knight manoeuvres via h7.

15 b3?!

White correctly hopes to enforce a3, b4, and open the queen-side where he has more space, but 15 Nf1 with the idea Ng3–f5 was more pertinent.

15 ... Nh7 16 Bf1 e4

Black takes as much central space as possible, though the move does shut in his queen's bishop, he hopes this pawn will be a spring-board for a king-side attack.

17 a3 Ng5 18 Qb2 Qf6 19 Be2 Qg6 20 Kh1 Qf5

White's last few moves have shown no direction (18 Qb2 19 Be2) so Black proceeds on the king-side. Indicated was 18 b4.

21 Rf1 Nf3

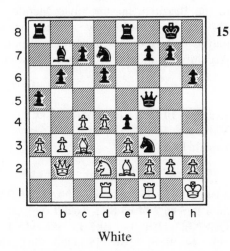

15

White

Black throws a "monkey wrench" into White's king-side, which of course cannot be accepted.

22 d5

White tries to shut the long diagonal avenue to his king while opening his own, but Black can rustle up a "posse".

22 ... Nde5 23 Bxe5 Nxe5 24 f3?

In search of counterplay White finally makes a serious error which can be blamed for his defeat. Correct was 24 Qc2 (pressuring and pinning the e-pawn) and then f3 or f4.

24 ... exf3 25 Nxf3?

White's lack of experience tells. His permanently backward e-pawn must spell defeat. Only 25 gxf3 offered dynamic chances.

25 ... Qe4 26 Nxe5 Rxe5 27 Rf3 Rae8 28 Bd3 Qh4

The rest of the game is now a so-called "matter of technique". Black piles up the e-pawn, White tries to counter on the f-file and king-side in general, but with a poor structure and little space to manoeuvre, this must fail.

29 Qd2 Bc8

The bishop's scope is greatly increased by this move.

30 Rf4 Qg5 31 Rdf1 f5!

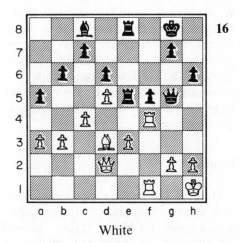

16

White

At first the decision to play this move was not an easy one, for the black bishop is made "bad" for no apparent reason; however, the activity and manoeuvring space of the major pieces and pawns takes precedence here. White's backward e-pawn is still awkward to defend while Black's f-pawn can be supported by ... g6.

32 h4 Qh5 33 Be2 Qf7 34 Bg4 Qf6 35 Qf2 g6

The result of this cat and mouse play between White's pieces and the black queen is that White is left with more weaknesses, Black has consolidated, and the e-pawn is still doomed.

36 h5 g5 37 Rxf5

Desperation. If 37 Rf3 Black can proceed quietly with 37 ... Kg7!, i.e. 38 Bxf5 Bxf5 39 Rxf5 Rxf5 40 Qxf5 Qxf5 41 Rxf5 Rxe3 42 Rf3 Rxf3 and Black wins the king and pawn ending; otherwise White soon runs out of moves.

37 ... Bxf5 38 Bxf5 Rf8 39 Bh7+?

A final blunder; much longer resistance was offered by 39 g4.

39 ... Kg7 40 Qxf6+ Rxf6 41 Rxf6 Kxf6 42 e4 Re8 White resigns.

During my 5 years in Britain I noticed that there is too much emphasis on prepared opening variations, particularly amongst young players, even strong ones. I do not really consider this to be normal chess. In the course of an "active" chess game every position should be considered on its own accord. The moves played should be an accumulation of your experience, knowledge, preparation and psychological state (feelings).

Example 9

Here is yet another example from the 12th Greater Manchester Open (Round 1) where I met Hutchinson (2120) who reeled off the first 11 "prepared" moves in 1 minute.

1 e4 Nc6 2 Nf3 d5 3 exd5 Qxd5 4 Nc3 Qa5 5 d4 Bg4 6 Bb5 0–0–0 7 Bxc6 bxc6 8 h3 Qh5 9 Qd3 Bxf3 10 gxf3 Rd6 11 Ne4 Re6.

I just took normal amounts of time, considered the threats, options, and problems of the position (since I'd never been in the variation before) to play:

12 Kf1

Now Black thought for 40 minutes and play continued:

12 ... Rg6 13 Bf4 e6 14 Qa6+ Kd7

I could not believe a good player would want to rush into Black's position and carefully thought over the thematic stroke:

15 d5! when after exd5 16 Qxa7 Qxf3 17 Qxc7+ Ke8 18 Qc8+ Ke7 19 Qb7+ Ke8 20 Qb8+ Kd7 21 Nc5+ Bxc5 22 Qc7+ Ke8 23 Re1+ Re6 24 Qxc6+ Ke7 25 Qxc5+ Kd7 26 Qc7+ Ke8 27 Rxe6+ fxe6 28 Rg1 Qxh3+ 29 Ke1 White soon won.

You can see that I had you, the reader, in mind in Manchester!

I must credit the following final example to the Brazilian master Silvio Mendes. In 1979 a 16-year-old boy named Amilcar played these moves against the well-known Argentine grandmaster, Miguel Quinteros:

Example 10 (Najdorf, Polugaevsky Variation, Rio de Janeiro, Brazil, 1979)

Amilcar–Quinteros

1 e4 c5 2 Nf3 d6 3 d4 cxd4 4 Nxd4 Nf6 5 Nc3 a6 6 Bg5 e6 7 f4 b5 8 e5 dxe5 9 fxe5 Qc7 10 Qe2 Nfd7 11 0–0–0 Bb7 12 Nf5 exf5 13 e6 Nf6 14 Bxf6 gxf6 15 Qh5 Bg7 (best 15 ... Bb4) 16 exf7+ Qxf7 17 Bxb5+! axb5 18 Rhe1+ Be4 19 Nxe4? (Winning is 19 Rd8+ Ke7 20 Nd5+ Ke6 21 Rd6+ Kxd6 22 Qxf7 Bxd5 23 Rd1) Qxh5?? 20 Ng5+ Black resigned.

A year earlier Amilcar had won a game in a Brazilian tournament with 19 Rd8+! in the position after 18 ... Be4. But after consulting Informant he rattled off these moves and played 19 Nxe4? according to its suggestion. Quinteros, a Najdorf expert, had forgotten the variation and was working out the moves over the board. However, his not playing 19 ... 0–0 even in time pressure, which was the logical, necessary and winning move, is inexcusable. Instead the grandmaster blundered, allowing 20 Ng5+ when mate follows.

References

Thought and Choice in Chess, by A. de Groot (Mouton Press).
Human Problem Solving, by A. Newell and H.A. Simon (Prentice-Hall).
Think Like a Grandmaster, by A. Kotov (Batsford).
The Best Move, by V. Hort and V. Jansa (R.H.M. Press).
Test Your Chess I.Q., by A. Livshitz (Pergamon Press).
Best Games of the Young Grandmasters, by C. Pritchett and D. Kopec (Bell & Hyman).

Lessons 9–12

HOW TO FORMULATE A PLAN

CHRIS MORRISON

INTRODUCTION

In the following four lessons I propose to examine various aspects of pawn structure and discuss the importance of open lines in all their forms. This course represents a mere "taste" of the underlying positional principles and keen readers should supplement it through studying the recommended texts and by gaining practical experience. However, this introduction will be devoted to explaining the importance of positional understanding and the way such knowleage can be applied in practice to formulate a plan.

When a player looks at a position and tries to determine the best way to continue, a decision may be relatively easy. For example there may exist a neat tactical combination to win material, or the chance to play for a direct mating attack. Such concepts are relatively easy to grasp and often will be neatly executed. But what should the player do if there is no obvious way to proceed? I have often heard players undertaking a "post-mortem" bemoaning the fact that "the books" say they had an edge, but they couldn't see what to do next, or that they "felt they stood better" but didn't know how to exploit their advantage.

Such problems arise due to a lack of understanding of the position and can be reduced through the gaining of positional experience consisting of a greater mental library of classic games and general principles. These precedents represent data upon which a positional assessment can be based and the plan of action determined. Most strong players will agree that in assessing an unfamiliar position, they will search their memory for analogies upon which to base their further play. It should be emphasized that their mental library will not necessarily contain a position which is similar in all, or even many, respects, but may contain an applicable tactical device, a game in which weak squares in the enemy position provided a springboard for attack, or some other piece of useful information. The extent to which players know which factors are vital in a given position depends on how highly developed their "intuitive" feel is. However, don't believe that such intuition is something you were either born with or will never have; it's a skill which can be trained and developed.

At this stage it is useful to outline the thought process which a master will use in determining a plan and then deciding upon the next move:

1. *The position will be assessed.* Account will be taken of the dominant positional factors such as pawn structure, open files and diagonals, and strong and weak squares.

2. *An objective will be determined.* On the basis of this assessment, the master may decide to, for example, pressurize a weakness, seize an open file, simplify to an advantageous endgame, etc.

3. *A plan will be conceived.* For example "I will double my rooks on the c-file, attempt to divert that knight from its defence of c7, and will then occupy the 7th rank with my rooks" or "I want to exchange off that black-squared bishop in order that the squares around the isolated pawn will be weakened."

4. *The plan will be executed.* Specific variations will be analysed until a way of carrying out the plan is found. It may emerge that the "ideal" plan fails tactically, in which case one which can be executed in the given position must be substituted.

The following lessons provide groundwork in positional assessment and determination of objectives, as a plan is merely a method of achieving the latter which is based on the former. I will not attempt to consider reams of tactical variations, nor will I attempt a comprehensive study of positional chess. Instead I will deal with a few fundamental themes and concepts, illustrated by examples, and direct the interested reader to further areas of study and sources of material.

LESSON 9

Basic Pawn Structures

Chess is a team game in the sense that if a player's pieces do not co-operate with each other in forming a well-deployed and co-ordinated force, all efforts are usually doomed to failure. Having quickly discovered that premature attacks using just one or two pieces are inadequate, a player will learn to place two pawns at e4 and d4, develop minor pieces, castle and centralize rooks before undertaking further action. This is very laudable, but soon it will be realized that it's not enough to blindly develop pieces without anchoring them on good squares. Given that the pawn structure adopted will play a vital role in determining the posts at which pieces will be actively placed and well co-ordinated, a good general principle is: "AIM FOR A PAWN STRUCTURE WHICH MAXIMISES FREEDOM AND STABILITY FOR YOUR PIECES, WHILE DENYING SIMILAR BENEFITS TO YOUR OPPONENT."

The preceding point, namely that the superiority of one player's structure is a measure of the inferiority of the opponent's, is an important one to bear in mind.

Diagram 1 shows what is known as the "classical" pawn formation, which has recurred for over 500 years.

White's formation is based on the premise that central control is a good thing. If pieces, especially minor pieces, are centrally posted, their scope is maximized, as they can be switched swiftly to either wing as the need arises. A strong pawn centre provides a firm foundation for such positioning. Thus White's pawns occupy e4 and d4, while attacking e5 and d5. Despite both sides having played just two moves in the diagrammed position, the strategic die has been cast for at least the next few moves. White has two pawns versus one in the centre and will develop pieces to active and aggressive squares. Black, on the other hand, established a central foothold with the e5 pawn and will develop defensively, re-

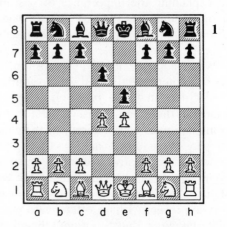

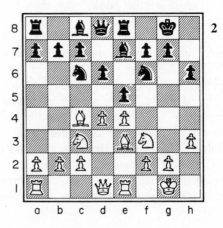

taining a solid, if rather cramped position with no concrete weaknesses.

Diagram 2 is an example of the kind of situation which may result. After the moves 1 e4 e5 2 Nf3 Nc6 3 Bc4 Be7 4 d4 d6 5 Nc3 Nf6 6 h3 (keeping Black cramped by denying access to g4) 6 ... 0–0 7 0–0 h6 8 Re1 Re8 9 Be3 the diagrammed position was reached. This provides a simple illustration of how the scope of pieces is determined by pawn structure, it being clear that Black's structure does not contain enough good squares to enable development to be completed. Indeed this idea of a player having too many pieces to "fit" the pawn structure is an important one. A good general rule is that in such positions the player with the space advantage should seek to preserve tension and avoid exchanges as in this way superior mobility may be exploited. It follows that the cramped player should try to gain freedom through exchanges. Thus Black continued 9 ... exd4 10 Nxd4 Bf8 11 Bf4 Nxd4 12 Qxd4 Be6. Although after 13 Rad1 White retained an edge with central pressure and more aggressive pieces, Black had avoided creating structural weaknesses.

While all the pieces can be redeployed if badly placed, this does not apply to pawns. Every time one is moved a definite change, for better or worse, will take place in the position. Pawns should not be thrown forward recklessly, without due consideration for the consequences, as while a deficit in development, or piece pressure for your opponent are mere temporary disadvantages, structural problems such as weak pawns and weak squares are permanent problems which can rarely be remedied in a satisfactory manner. A good example of excessive pawn pushing was Antoshin–Ivkov, in which after Black's 9th move Diagram 3 was reached, while after Black's 17th move Diagram 4 arose.

In Diagram 3 White has a huge space advantage and has active prospects on both king- and queen-side. He will obviously be able to switch his pieces from wing to wing much faster than Black whose pieces are in a

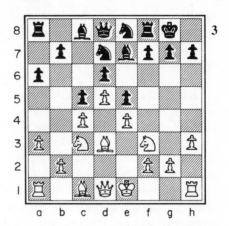

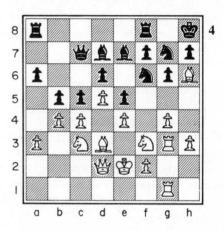

traffic jam on his back two ranks. However Black's position has no concrete weaknesses, whereas there's a chance that White's advanced pawns may become exposed. Antoshin proceeds to overextend in every direction simultaneously and accordingly reaches the brink of collapse in just 8 more moves! The game continued, 10 g4 g6 11 Bh6 Ng7 12 b4?! b6 13 Qd2 Nf6 14 Ke2 Kh8 15 Rag1 Bd7 16 Rg3 Qc7 17 Rhg1 b5!

Diagram 4 has now been reached and suddenly White's queen-side caves in. He can't capture twice on b5, as e4 will end up hanging, but the whole queen-side is about to open up, leaving his position riddled with weaknesses. In despair Antoshin tried 18 h4, but soon lost horribly 18 ... bxc4 19 Bc2 (Not 19 Bxc4?? cxb4 winning a piece) 19 ... cxb4 20 axb4 Rab8 21 h5 Rxb4 22 hxg6 fxg6 23 Rh1 Rb2 24 Kd1 Qa5 25 Ng5

Nxg4 26 Bxg7+ Kxg7 27 Rxh7+ Kg8 28 Qc1 Bxg5 29 Qxg5 Qa1+ and White resigned. A drastic example of the risks of over-zealous pawn pushing!

A general definition of a "weak pawn" is: "one which cannot be defended by another pawn". Such pawns are weak because (1) they depend upon pieces for protection and are easily lost, (2) by tying down pieces to their defence they may leave their possessor vulnerable to aggression elsewhere on the board, (3) weak pawns tend to have weak squares around them which may provide the opponent with strong outposts for pieces, or lead to weak colour complexes, concepts which will be central to Lesson 10. I shall end this lesson with examples of common types of pawn weakness.

Isolated Pawn

An isolated pawn is simply one which has no pawn of its own colour on an adjacent file to give it support. Such a pawn some-times gives dynamic chances in a middle-game, but represents a long-term structural weakness which will be a particular liability in an endgame.

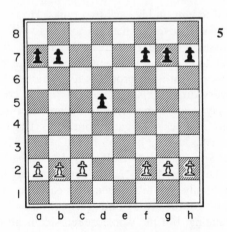

Its vulnerability will be especially marked when, as in Diagram 5, it lies on a half-open file and is exposed to direct attack by both rooks and minor pieces. Futhermore, the square in front of an isolated pawn will always be a beautiful outpost on which enemy pieces can be established. The reader may consider that as long as Black is able to defend this pawn as often as it's attacked, there is little to fear. Unfortunately, in practice it's often hard to guard against threats elsewhere, while still protecting the pawn adequately.

An excellent example of overstretching an opponent who is nursing a structural defect was given by the Russian master Kan (Diagram 6).

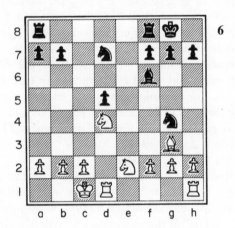

It's not enough for White to attack the d-pawn with as many pieces as possible, since Black can defend likewise, but his ability to dictate the course of the game proves decisive: 16 Nf3 Nb6 17 h3 Nh6 18 Nf4 Rfd8 19 Rd3 Rd7 20 Rhd1 Rad8 (Black threatens to reactivate his knight by Nf5, but . . .) 21 Bh2!! (Excellent — if now 21 ... Nf5 22 g4 and the threat of 23 g5 forces 22 ... Nd6, and the d-pawn falls) 21 ... g6 22 g4 Bg7 23 Bg3! (threatening 24 Bh4, hitting the rook on d8) 23 ... f6 (This would soon have been forced, but now e6 is weak too) 24 Nd4! Nf7 25 Nde6 Ne5 26 Nxd8! Nxd3+ 27 Nxd3! Rxd8 28 Nc5 — the point. White's queen-side thrust is the final blow and the b-pawn falls. Although a tactical trick finally won material, Black never really looked like surviving against Kan's skilful manoeuvres.

Backward pawn

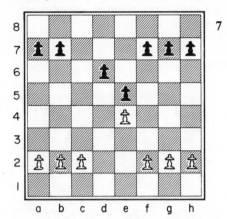

As can be seen from Diagram 7, a "backward pawn" is one which has lost the support of its neighbours by lagging behind and has consequently become weak. If readers add doubled white rooks on the d-file and visualize a knight arriving on b5, they will realize the kind of direct pressure to which the pawn may be subjected. Note that the threat of Nb5 in such positions often forces ... a6 weakening Black's queen-side dark squares, especially b6. In practice Black can usually guard the d6 pawn against direct attack based on a "weight of numbers" concept, but White exploits the fact that Black is tied to defence by generating great central and queen-side pressure, often hinged around a dominant knight on the desperately weak d5 square. Add a white knight on d5, place the respective a-pawns on a5 and a6, and it does not require a positional genius to see that Black's game is bad.

Doubled pawn

Unlike isolated pawns and backward pawns, which are virtually always structurally bad, doubled pawns are only usually bad. Of course, structural monstrosities like doubled isolated pawns are terrible and represent easy endgame targets. However, doubled pawns supported by an adjacent pawn have considerable defensive strength,

as they cover many squares. The problem is that if the need to use them actively arises, they are only marginally more forcing than a single pawn as they impede each other.

Consider the following diagrams (Diagrams 8, 9 and 10).

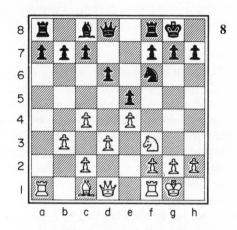

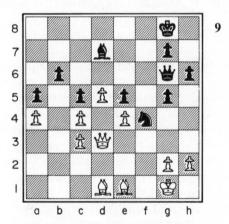

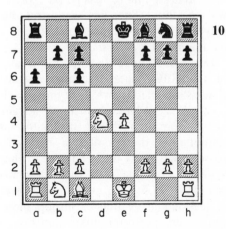

Diagram 8 arises from a line in the Bishop's opening favoured by Larsen and is a position in which the doubled pawn complex actually gives White an edge. Pieces will fit nicely into the pawn structure, the opposing bishop is restrained and the base of the structure at c2 is very safe. Furthermore, White almost has an extra centre pawn as one of the c-pawns is often exchanged for Black's d-pawn.

Diagram 9 comes from a famous win by Fischer over Spassky in their 1972 match. The position is structurally interesting, as despite Black's backward b-pawn on a half-open file, his isolated e-pawn and his doubled g-pawns, and despite White having a protected passed pawn and the bishop pair, Black has a clear advantage. To understand this it is necessary to appreciate that neither Black's b-pawn nor his e-pawn can be attacked easily, White's d-pawn is restrained, and his a-pawn is weak. In addition Black has a fine knight on f4 which is an "effective outpost", as to dislodge it by g3 would desperately weaken White's king-side white squares. However, the key to White's problems is his doubled pawn complex, c3/c4. Such doubled and effectively isolated pawns are often directly vulnerable, but in this position they are weak because they strangle White by killing all hope of active play, his bishops being totally passive. The game ended dramatically: 27 Qc2?? (27 Qb1 is forced when White can struggle on) 27 ... Bxa4 White resigns (If 28 Qxa4 Qxe4 wins instantly). Such games illustrate how a player must appreciate which factors are paramount in a *particular* position.

Diagram 10 arises from an old treatment of the Ruy Lopez Exchange Variation. Black's doubled pawns are not weak in themselves, White's structural advantage arising from the fact that Black's formation cannot force the creation of a queen-side passed pawn in the endgame, whereas White's "workable" 4–3 king-side majority can easily do so. The position is, however, at least equal as Black's bishop pair can prove very powerful, in conjunction with

pressure from centralized rooks. There is thus sufficient dynamic compensation for the structural deficiency.

Hanging pawns

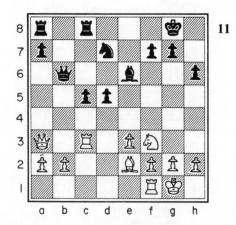

Diagram 11 is a situation in which Black has hanging pawns at c5 and d5. Clearly such pawns are a powerful force if they can be maintained side by side, controlling many important squares. In certain circumstances the d-pawn may advance and become a powerful passed pawn. Indeed, in positions with more minor pieces on the board, the thrust ... d4 attacking a piece with tempo, followed by ... c4 with tempo, then ... d3, establishing a protected passed pawn, has claimed many victims. White must keep the pawns under careful restraint to avoid such possibilities. The pawns often become a liability if, for instance, White manages to exchange e- for d-pawn leaving Black with a weak isolated c-pawn. Alternatively, the c-pawn may be forced to advance leaving a backward d-pawn on a half-open file, or the d-pawn may be forced to advance in a situation in which the passed pawn created is merely isolated and weak.

A general rule to apply for hanging pawns is the following: "if they can be maintained side by side, or advanced ON THE POSSESSOR'S TERMS, they may be strong, but if the opponent can force their advance, or liquidate one of them they're probably weak".

LESSON 10

**Pawn Islands, Outposts, and
Colour Complexes**

Pawn Islands

In the course of a game pawns which
started in a united chain of 8 usually get
separated into sub-chains, gaps being
caused by the exchange of some of them.
An important principle, with particular
relevance in the endgame, is that the player
with the fewer "pawn islands" (Capablanca's name for these sub-chains) has a
structural plus. Often the player with more
islands has obvious weaknesses such as
isolated pawns, but consider Diagram 12.

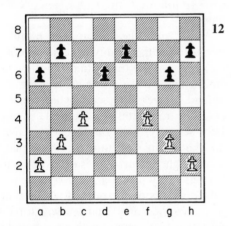

Each side has 6 pawns, none of which are
backward or isolated, but White's pawns are
in two islands of three each, whereas Black's
are in three islands of two. It follows that
White has a positional edge, having three
targets for attack (at b7, e7, and h7 being
the base of each sub-chain) while Black has
only two such targets.

That was a very simple example, but
within my experience, the relative number
of pawn islands is always an important and
sometimes a decisive endgame factor, something which students should verify by playing through master endgames with island
imbalance. For the present, I warn the

student to be aware of this concept, when
conceiving middlegame plans, for it is at this
stage in the game that the endgame pawn
structure is often decided.

Outposts

In discussing isolated and backward
pawns I emphasized the weak squares in
front of them, indicating that such outposts
are as much, and often more, of a problem
for the weaker side as the weakness of the
pawn itself. An outpost may be defined as
"a useful square where one can establish
pieces which CANNOT BE ATTACKED BY
ENEMY PAWNS". The key points are that the
square can only be contested by enemy
pieces and that it is USEFUL, which implies a
central square or a foothold in the enemy
position. It should be relevantly placed to be
a platform for attack, a lynchpin for co-
ordination of the player's own forces, a
disruptive weapon against your opponent's
co-ordination, or a combination of some or
all of these factors.

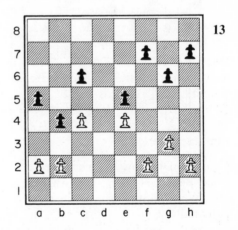

Consider Diagram 13. This pawn structure, arising from an Old Indian defence in
which White has erroneously played c4 gives
Black two useful outposts, on c5 and d4,
which cannot be challenged by white pawns.
If readers visualize knights (the knight being
the super-piece of outpost play) established

on these squares, it is clear that they would dominate the board. The white queen-side would be under direct pressure which could be increased by pawn advances, while Black would control the centre and could switch pressure to the king-side too if necessary. In contrast, White has no such squares on which to anchor pieces and is condemned to a life of defensive drudgery. To retain control of the position, Black must avoid a pawn of either colour reaching c5. Playing ... c5 would mean that each side had one good square (d4 for Black, d5 for White). To allow White to play c5 would be even worse, as then b6, c4 and d6 would become valuable outposts while Black would only control d4. The lesson to be learned is "guard your structural advantages carefully".

The usefulness of outposts is a key factor, as the point of controlling them is to further one's cause elsewhere.

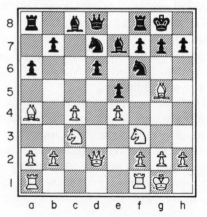

Consider Diagram 14, which arose in the game Benko–Najdorf, Los Angeles, 1963, after White's 14th move. White clearly has a potentially strong outpost on f5, but Black now multiplied his own problems with the positional blunder 14 ... Bxf3? (He should have played ... Na6, but was probably afraid of 15 Nh2). His object was to secure his own knight on its advanced square f4, but if White castles queen-side, this piece will attack thin air. In addition, by giving up his white-squared bishop, Black destroys his own chances of disputing White's domi-

nation of f5. The game continued: 15 gxf3 Nd7 16 0–0–0 (naturally) 16 ... Re8 17 Bh3 (White simply threatens Bf5 followed by doubling rooks on the h-file and manoeuvring his knight to e3, a plan which would soon be decisive. Black must therefore remove this bishop. Note in passing that Bxf4 by White at any stage would merit "??" as Black would reply exf4 and gain access to the beautiful squares d4 and e5) 17 ... Nxh3 18 Rxh3 Nf8 19 Rah1 Ng6 20 Nd1 Rc8 21 Ne3 Rc7 22 Nf5 (A fine example of a dominant knight outpost in a very useful place!) 22 ... Rf8 23 Qd1 f6 (Black has no chance of holding this position in the long run, but White now achieves a quick tactical kill) 24 f4! exf4 25 Qh5 Ne5 (If 25 ... fxg3 26 Qxg6 followed by Rh8 mate) 26 Qh7+ Black resigned (26 ... Kf7 27 Qxg7+ Ke8 28 Qxf8+ followed by Rh8+ and Rxd8 is fatal).

Aside from the lesson that usefulness, that is to say the quality of outposts not just their quantity, is important, another point emerging from the above game is that if the defender gives up pieces which have the potential to contest an outpost, it tempts fate severely. An outpost can only be attacked by pieces; thus it follows that the way to fight against one, is to cover it with at least as many pieces as your opponent uses to support its occupation. If it's then occupied, a series of exchanges will force the possessor to recapture with a pawn and lose access to the square.

In Diagram 15 White has a fine outpost at d5, but Black forced its occupation by a pawn through some neat tactics. Play continued: 1 ... Nb6 2 Bb3 Bg4 3 Ne1 Rc8 4 Qd3 Be6 5 Bxf6 (forced) Bxf6 6 Nd5 (forced) 6 ... Nxd5 7 exd5 and the outpost was just a memory. In the event that such a defence is impossible, standard methods are to exchange off your opponent's most potent occupying pieces, or, if this is also unachievable, to seek active counterplay elsewhere.

Finally, I would ask readers to be aware of the possibility of "building" outposts in their games, whether by forcing weaknesses in the enemy position, or by advancing pawns to support pieces. Such advances must be judged carefully, and the risks weighed against the potential benefits, but outpost building can often provide a plan when you feel yourself drifting and should always be borne in mind.

Black squares and white squares: Colour complexes

Readers will doubtless have heard the expression that one player is weak on the black/white squares. This could mean, for example, that the pawn structure in the area of the board in question, say the king-side, is such that these pawns are on white squares and do not adequately defend a group of black squares. In such situations the player with what we shall call a "weak colour complex" will often have difficulty in resisting an attack which aims to break through on, or infiltrate via, the weak squares. The problem of defence will be vastly increased if the defensive bishop which operates on squares of the same colour as the weak squares has been exchanged, as this will make it much harder to protect the holes in the pawn structure.

It is best to illustrate what is meant diagrammatically (see Diagram 16).
Black has a standard fianchettoed king-side and it's clear that although the pawns don't

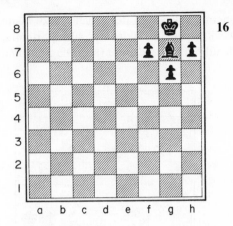

defend the black squares f6, g5, and h6, the bishop is performing this task, while moves such as ... f6 or ... h6 are possible if necessary. Now imagine that the black-squared bishops have been exchanged, removing Black's bishop on g7. Suddenly the king-side black squares look rather exposed, and if a white pawn is added on e5, together with a black pawn on e6, and it's assumed that white pieces are preventing ... h6, it's easy to envisage white pieces swarming in for the kill via f6 and h6. This is why an almost invariable stage in attacking a fianchettoed position is the exchange of the bishop which defends the potentially weak squares.

Obviously the addition of a black white-squared bishop in the previous example would do nothing to cover the weaknesses, and this introduces the idea of the "bad bishop". When a player has numerous pawns on squares of one colour, a bishop of the opposite colour, such as the fianchettoed bishop in the diagram, is "good". It has great freedom and covers those squares which the pawns don't. Conversely, if a player with one bishop left commits the common "beginner's error" of placing pawns on squares of the same colour as that bishop, in the mistaken belief that they'll be defended and safe, this will greatly impede its freedom. Furthermore, it will be found that since squares of the opposite colour are neither protected by pawns nor bishop, the enemy will infiltrate. Such "bad bishop/ weak square" syndromes are particularly deadly in the endgame (see Diagram 17).

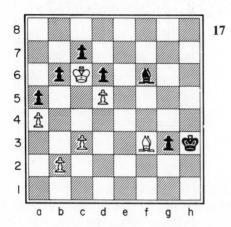

McNab–Sowray, London, 1982

The diagrammed position was the culmination of a gradual "swindle". Black had been winning comfortably but allowed his queen-side pawns to be lured on to black squares with the result that the white king infiltrated via the unprotected white squares c4 and b5 to its dominating position at c6. 49 ... Bd8 would be futile after 50 Kd7, so Black continued 49 ... g2 50 Bxg2+ Kxg2 with an extra piece. Nevertheless, White won comfortably after 51 Kxc7 Kf3 52 Kxb6 Bd8+ 53 Kc6 Ke4 54 Kxd6 Kd3 55 Kc5 Kc2 56 b4 Kb3 57 Kb5 Kxc3 58 bxa5 and Black resigned.

Given that in the endgame the king can operate freely on squares of both colours, a good measure of endgame colour complex weaknesses is to assess the ease with which the enemy king can infiltrate. If the answer is easily, remedial measures should be undertaken immediately. Knights, like kings, have the capacity for play on squares of both colours, so one should be aware of the possibility of liquidating to a "good knight versus bad bishop" endgame. These generally feature a cramped bishop, grovelling behind a badly arranged pawn structure, while its king tries to fight off both the

enemy king and knight. A combination of diversionary attacks and king manoeuvres gives the knight many victories in such situations.

I have discussed weak colour complexes in the context of the endgame as it's there that the problems can be illustrated most clearly. However, one must be aware that such weaknesses can be deadly in the middlegame too. There are frequent examples in master play of attacking strategies based on squares of one colour. To conclude this lesson, here is a drastic example of dark square strategy by a player who pioneered understanding of such plans, Aron Nimzowitsch.

In the game Nimzowitsch–Miss Menchik, Carlsbad, 1929, the position in Diagram 18 arose after Black's 9th move.

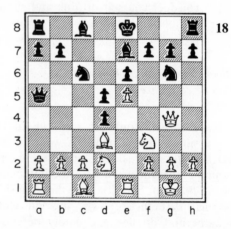

White continued: 10 h4! Bf8 11 h5 Nge7 12 Nb3 Qc7 13 Nbxd4 Nxd4 14 Nxd4 Bd7 15 Bg5 (White has already established a powerful bind, with a strong knight on d4 and cramping pawns on e5 and h5. Black must also defend against penetration to the d6 outpost. Moreover Black's king has no safe refuge. By 15 Bg5 White threatens Bxe7 and it's hard for Black to avoid 15 ... g6 furthering White's coming black square attack) Black continued 15 ... g6 16 Rac1 Nf5 17 Bf6 Rg8 18 Bxf5 exf5 19 Qe2 Qb6 20 c3 Bc5 21 b4 Bxd4 (Hopeless, but Black is totally lost — either she gets crushed by a breakthrough supported by White's dominant knight, or she gets crushed on her weak black squares after giving up her black-squared bishop as in the game) 22 cxd4 Be6 (Trying to blockade the centre) 23 Rc5! (Black is surrounded on the black squares) 23 ... Kd7 24 Qf3 Qxb4 (desperation) 25 Rxd5+ Ke8 26 Rc1 Bxd5 27 Qxd5 Qb6 28 Qf3 gxh5 29 Qa3 Qe6 30 Rc7 Black resigned. Having been held in a total bind on them, Black is now mated on the black squares (see Diagram 19).

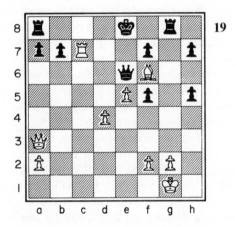

Thus two important basic rules are:

1. If you have one bishop left AVOID PLACING YOUR PAWNS ON THE SAME COLOURED SQUARES AS IT.
2. Generally avoid pawn chains on squares of one colour if this means the creation of VULNERABLE weak squares of the other colour.

LESSON 11

Open Lines — Part I

Open lines can take various forms, these being OPEN FILES, HALF-OPEN FILES, and DIAGONALS. The open diagonal can be a potent weapon and is a vital component of many openings, as exemplified by Black's fianchettoed bishop in the Sicilian Dragon

and by the latent energy of Black's fianchettoed bishop in some variations of the King's Indian Defence. It can spring into the game with devastating effect if the h8–a1 diagonal is opened (see Diagram 20).

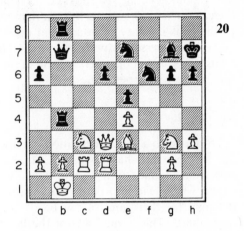

NN–Kotov

In this position Kotov, having already opened and seized control of the b-file and undermined White's centre, activated his remaining pieces — in particular his black-squared bishop — by opening the long black diagonal. He struck with 28 ... d5! and after 29 exd5 (29 Bc5 gives more chances) 29 ... e4! the bishop came into its own. The game ended 30 Qe2 Nexd5 (threatening Nxc3, followed by Nd5 and carnage on b2) 31 Nd1 Nd7 32 Rc4 Rxc4 33 Qxc4 Nxe3 34 Nxe3 Bxb2 35 Qb3 Bg7 36 Rxd7 Qxd7 37 Qxb8 Qd3+ 38 Kc1 (If 38 Nc2 Qd1 mate) 38 ... Qxe3+ White resigned.

Most readers will have played or seen games in which a battery of bishops at, for example, d3 and e3 bear down on the enemy king-side. It's possible to cite openings such as the Modern Defence (1 e4 g6 2 d4 Bg7) in which one player makes no effort to occupy the centre but instead hopes to attack it later by pawn moves supported by raking bishop(s). A good general rule is to place bishops on open diagonals in order to maximize their scope. Bishops are usually at their best in open positions, so always bear in mind the possibility of opening lines for them.

While a bishop on an open diagonal which points at enemy weaknesses can be a potent weapon in co-operation with other pieces, infiltration, generally by rooks, on an open file can often be decisive in its own right due to the rook's ability to attack and destroy enemy weaknesses, especially pawns. This leads to discussion of a second form of open line, namely the open file.

The open file

To start with a simple definition, an open file is one which has no pawns of either colour on it. Such files represent two-way streets which lead into both positions, thus the fight for their control can be of great importance. This is the basis of the beginner's rule: "place rooks on open files". Indeed, the rook can be a devastating piece when played into attacking positions via an open file as numerous powerful plans may become possible.

Before discussing the important themes of control, penetration, targets and disruptive power, here is a classic example of rooks penetrating via an open file and, in this case, doubling on the 7th rank with devastating effect.

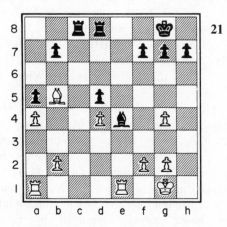

Karpov–Uhlmann, Madrid 1973

Diagram 21 arose after Black's 24th move in a French Defence, Karpov having just liquidated into an advantageous endgame. Both the c- and e-files are open and White's control of the e-file is guaranteed by his well-posted bishop at b5, which by controlling e8 will stop Black contesting the file. White's bishop may later move to e8 to assist in attacking f7, in contrast to Black's, which will be forced onto the passive square g6 and will not even be able to maintain that defensive position. On the other hand, Black controls the c-file and can penetrate via c2 with counterplay, so why is White better? The answer to this question is the key to the modern understanding of open files and gives rise to a very important rule which it is essential to grasp: "AN OPEN FILE HAS NO SIGNIFICANCE IN ITSELF AND IS IMPORTANT ONLY IF IT CAN BE USED FOR SOME STRATEGIC PURPOSE". Karpov realizes that the e-file is the more valuable as (1) he will penetrate to e7 before Black reaches c2; (2) he will force the doubling of his rooks on the 7th rank, while restraining Black's counterplay by a latent threat of back rank mate which gains a tempo; (3) he will then have a target on f7, the fall of which will create mating threats; (4) Black will be unable to defend passively, as White will dislodge his pieces by pawn advances and the dominant rooks on the 7th will make effective defensive co-ordination impossible; (5) if Black tries to play actively and counter-attack, he will have insufficiently mortal targets and leave himself fatally exposed.

Now observe how Karpov pressed home his advantage: 25 f3 (clearing the way to the 7th) 25 ... Bg6 26 Re7 (attacking b7 with gain of tempo) 26 ... b6 27 Rae1! (gaining another tempo, for if 27 ... Rc2 28 Re8+ forces mate) 27 ... h6 28 Rb7 Rd6 (Black tries to defend, but counter-attacking by 28 ... Rc2 also fails as his king becomes fatally exposed, e.g. 29 R1e7 Rxb2 30 Be8 Rc8 31 Bxf7+ Bxf7 32 Rxf7 R8c2 33 Rxg7+ Kf8 34 Kh2! and now White's king escapes but Black's is hopelessly placed, for example 34 ... Rxg2+ 35 Kh3 Rh2+ 36 Kg3 Rhg2+ 37 Kf4 Rb4 38 Rh7 Kg8 39 Rhd7 winning) 29 R1e7 h5 30 gxh5 Bxh5 31 g4

Bg6 32 f4! (Karpov's plan continues as he prepares to dislodge the bishop from its defence of f7) 32 ... Rc1+ 33 Kf2 Rc2+ 34 Ke3 Be4 (f7 was indefensible) 35 Rxf7 Rg6 36 g5 (engineering the collapse of g7) 36 ... Kh7 37 Rfe7 Rxb2 38 Be8 Rb3+ 39 Ke2 Rb2+ 40 Ke1 Rd6 41 Rxg7+ Kh8 42 Rge7 Black resigned. (When his check runs out he will have no defence to White's threats, e.g. Rb8 followed by bishop moves mate, or if Black plays ... Rd8 simply g6 wins.)

Perfect examples such as this tend to give players delusions of simplicity. They think that if a rook is established on an open file, victory will surely follow, but consider the position in Diagram 22:

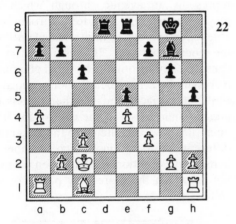

22

Black has just played Rad8 "occupying" the open d-file but he's lost! White plays 1 Be3 attacking the a-pawn and after 1 ... a6 (if 1 ... b6 2 a5 c5 3 axb6 axb6 4 Ra6 Black's queen-side collapses) 2 Bb6 Rd7 3 Rad1 R8e7 (3 ... Rde7 4 Bd8! followed by Rd7 wins) 4 Bc5 Rxd1 5 Rxd1 Re8 (5 ... Rc7? 6 Rd8+ Kh7 7 Bd6 is embarrassing!) 6 Rd7 winning easily. That position was a simple example of the need to be able to penetrate on an open file. Black was unable to do so as White's king was well-placed to stop any entry while, when the file changed hands (the "two-way street" theme) White effected a decisive penetration via d7.

The fight for control of an open file or files is a vital phase in many games, with players doubling rooks or even trebling the rooks and their queen. Minor pieces may play an important role by controlling key squares (see Karpov–Uhlmann) or through diversionary attacks as in Example 2. The decision to contest an open file may be defensive as a player tries to protect weaknesses, or aggressive in trying to attack those of the opponent. However, before such operations are embarked upon it's vital to assess the usefulness of the file, or indeed the relative importance of different files in the context of the particular position.

The following factors should be considered in making such an assessment:

1. *Control.* This will tend to be a case of who can ultimately bring more firepower to bear on the file. Although control will sometimes pass on a "first come, first served" basis, we have already seen how a file may change hands when the initial occupant fails to maintain his presence.

2. *Penetration. In the event that control of a file may be won, one must establish whether there exists a point on it at which the enemy position can be penetrated.* Such an "entry square" will usually be on the 7th rank, although sometimes on the 6th or 8th, and will be a square which cannot be defended by enemy pawns. It will often be defended by enemy pieces and the potential to exchange such defenders off or drive/divert them away must exist. If, however, all the possible entry squares are securely defended, the value of the open file is greatly diminished.

3. *Targets.* In the event that penetration on the open file is possible, are there targets for attack within the enemy camp? Typical targets are pawns which have been outflanked and may be attacked from the side and/or from behind. In many cases the open file will lead to one or two rooks being established on the 7th rank and co-ordinating with other pieces to make targets of enemy pieces, or even of the enemy king.

4. *Disruptive power.* This relates to the idea of targets, but is more subtle in that the file may, in some cases, not lead to win of

material or direct attack. The opponent may be tied down to such an extent that a decisive blow can be delivered elsewhere. An excellent example of penetration on an open file paralysing the opposition is Stahlberg–Taimanov, Zurich Candidates, 1953.

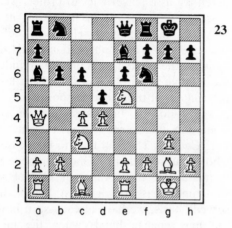

Diagram 23 arose after White's 10th move and Taimanov seized the initiative with 10 ... b5! (This forces the creation of an open c-file, over which Black gains control by exchanging off White's best pieces and forcing the rest back in confusion. Meanwhile he smoothly develops his own forces on good squares, creating a potent, well-coordinated force.) Play continued: 11 cxb5 cxb5 12 Qd1 b4 13 Nb1 Nc6 14 Nxc6 Qxc6 (Black is well on the way to control of the c-file and the beautiful entry square, c2, already beckons) 15 Nd2 Qb6 16 e3 Rac8 17 Bf1 Rc6 18 Bxa6 Qxa6 19 Nf3 Rfc8 20 Qb3 Ne4 21 Nd2 (otherwise f2 will be fatally weak after Rc2. Now Black could have won two pieces for a rook by 21 ... Rxc1 but decides that his paralysing grip on White's position is more deadly). Black continued 21 ... Rc2! 22 Nxe4 dxe4 23 a3 h5! (excellent — White can scarcely move, so Black launches a king-side attack based on the weak king-side white squares and White's inability to feed pieces over for defence without making fatal concessions elsewhere) 24 d5 (White is becoming desperate) 24 ... R8c4! (killing any hope of simplification. If now 25 dxe6 Qxe6 threatening

26 ... Rxc1 27 Raxc1 Rxc1 28 Qxe6 Rxe1+! in addition to king-side mating threats, leaving White hopelessly placed) 25 Rd1 exd5 26 Bd2 Qf6 27 Rab1 h4 28 Qa4 Qf5 29 Qxa7 Bf8(?) (29 ... Bg5 would give Black a mating attack, but now White managed to exchange queens, although into a lost endgame which Taimanov soon won).

The discussion of open lines will continue in Lesson 12 which deals with half-open files.

LESSON 12

Half-Open Files

In Lesson 11 we saw how an open file represents an avenue through which the player who wins the fight for control may be able to feed pieces, to infiltrate and outflank the enemy position. It was necessary to consider, among other factors, whether control could be achieved, whether penetration could take place, and whether targets for attack would exist. In the case of the half-open file, however, there are fundamentally different considerations, which are inherent in the very definition of a half-open file as "a file on which there are only pawns of one colour".

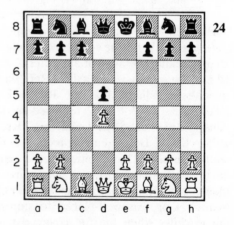

In Diagram 24, which originates from the Exchange Variation of the Queen's Gambit Declined, two half-open files have been created as early as move three. These are

the c-file which will be controlled by White and the e-file which will be controlled by Black. After e3 by White and c6 by Black, both sides will be free to attack along "their" open files. This is the keystone of White's strategy in this variation, although for reasons discussed later, Black's counter-play does not tend to come through pressure on e3. The points to be made at this stage are, firstly, that a half-open file can be dominated by the side with no pawn on it, without there being any practical chances of the file changing hands, or even being contested effectively. If the black c-pawn is moved to c6 in the diagram, and the reader imagines White playing a rook to c1, it's obvious that Black would have to go through contortions to oppose it directly by placing a rook on c4! Furthermore, when one attacks on a half-open file, there will be a ready-made object of attack at the end of it.

All this sounds very favourable, but there's another side to the half-open file coin. Whereas in the case of an open file it was necessary to penetrate via an empty square, it is now necessary to attack an enemy pawn. This may be relatively easy if the pawn is weak, whether backward or isolated, but if it's defended by another pawn, the attack may "bite on granite". It may then be necessary to consider a piece sacrifice when attacking the king, or where the object is to force weaknesses, to undertake the undermining operation known as the "MINORITY ATTACK" which will be discussed shortly.

In the lesson on weak pawns examples were given of how backward and isolated pawns are particularly weak if they lie on a half-open file. They are exposed to direct attack, which means that pieces may be tied down to their defence. Therefore a player should be alert to the possibilities of opening a file to expose such a weakness.

Diagram 25 arose after Black's 8th move, in the game Morrison–Povah, British Championship, 1978, and White, despite having expended a tempo on 5 d3, played 9

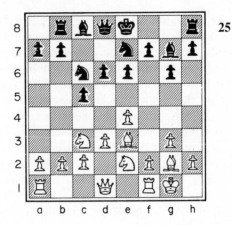

d4! The positional point of this move is that if Black captures on d4, he will find himself with a weak backward pawn on the freshly-opened d-file. While a pawn on d6 is not often a weakness in the Sicilian Defence, in the diagrammed position Black has played e6 and fianchettoed his king's bishop. Thus with the d-file opened, he will be hard-pressed to defend d6. For example, after 9 ... cxd4 10 Nxd4 a6 (otherwise 11 Ndb5 would be crushing) Black is clearly worse with a backward, exposed d-pawn and weak queen-side black squares. Aside from the positional merits of 9 d4, it's a good example of the effect the "exception to a rule", in this case the one which says that pieces (in this case "pieces" include pawns) shouldn't be moved twice in the opening, can have. As far as Black was concerned, White was committed to a closed game and his defensive set-up was based on this assumption. The moral behind this is "think flexibly".

In the game Black declined to make the d-file half-open and continued 9 ... b6, but after 10 Qd2 0–0 11 Rad1 Ba6 12 Rfe1, he felt obliged by White's threatened central breakthrough to play 12 ... cxd4. However, after 13 Nxd4 White's superior co-ordination, together with his pressure on the d-file, led to a decisive advantage: 13 ... Ne5 14 b3 Ng4 15 Bg5 Rc8 16 h3 Nf6 17 Ndb5 Ne8 18 e5! (thematic and decisive — White soon won).

In a situation where the target pawn will be supported by another pawn, a minority attack may be possible. Viewed in simple terms, the objective when a- and b-pawns face a-, b-, and c-pawns will be to eliminate all but the c-pawn, on the basis that it will then be unsupported and weak.

A typical example of the power of such a plan in the absence of effective counterplay, was seen in the game van Den Berg–Kramer, 1950, in which after the opening moves: 1 d4 Nf6 2 c4 e6 3 Nc3 d5 4 Bg5 Be7 5 Nf3 0–0 6 Qc2 Nbd7 7 cxd5 exd5 8 e3 c6 9 Bd3 Re8 10 0–0 Nf8 11 Rab1, Diagram 26 was reached.

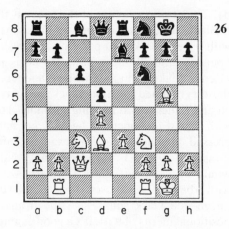

26

Black continued 11 ... g6 (this starts a plan aimed at exchanging White-squared bishops, but it's far too slow; 11 ... Ne4! is better) 12 b4 a6 13 a4 Ne6 14 Bh4 Ng7 15 b5 axb5 16 axb5 Bf5 17 bxc6 bxc6 (White's strategy has produced a weak backward pawn on c6, its support having been undermined). 18 Ne5 (he attacks the weakness immediately) 18 ... Rc8 19 Rb7 (note that as well as the weak target on c6, the minority attack has also created open files which can be used for infiltration and outflanking manoeuvres) 19 ... Bxd3 20 Qxd3 Rc7 21 Rxc7 Qxc7 22 Rc1 (threatening 23 Bxf6 Bxf6 24 Nxd5 winning) 22 ... Qb7 23 Qb1 Qa6 (If 23 ... Qxb1 24 Nxb1 and the c-pawn falls) 24 Na2 and the c-pawn falls, e.g. 24 ... Rc8 25 Bxf6 Bxf6 26 Nb4 etc.

There are many examples of such minority attacks leading to an almost "automatic" win, but the reader may wonder why Black doesn't undertake similar operations against White's e3 pawn by playing ... f5, ... f4, in co-operation with ... g5 if necessary. The answer is that Black's king would be left exposed to an extent which White's is not justified by the possible creation of one or two pawn weaknesses in White's position. However, it's possible for Black to create sufficient counter-chances by active king-side piece play.

In addition to the Exchange Variation of the Queen's Gambit Declined, there are several other openings which create half-open files, together with a pawn structure featuring minority attack potential. Several lines in the English Opening do this but perhaps the most important example is the Sicilian Defence. Consider the following two diagrams:

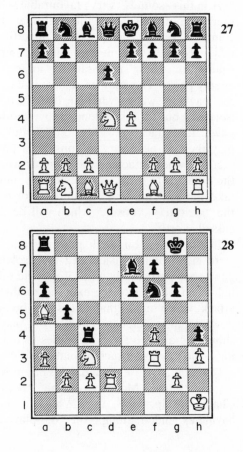

27

28

In Diagram 27 Black has already obtained a half-open c-file, a central pawn majority and the potential for a minority attack which will saddle White with a weak c-pawn. In the short term White has a lead in development and fine attacking chances, which means that many Sicilian Defences develop along explosive lines with piece sacrifices flying about, and the result of the game hinging on the success or failure of White's king-side attack. The positional justification for the Sicilian Defence does, however, lie in Black's long-term structural advantage. Therefore it's important that players should not merely learn long "book" variations, but should also be aware of the vital underlying themes.

In Diagram 28 Andersson, a player who likes "long-term" advantages, has reached a very favourable Sicilian ending. White's problems on the c-file, in conjunction with his weak f4 pawn, give Black a clear plus. After 24 b3 Rc6 25 a4 b4 26 Ne2 Rac8, White was reduced to 27 c4 but after 27 ... bxc3 28 Rxc3 Nd5 his weaknesses on b3 and f4 proved fatal.

In undertaking an attack against the enemy king, players will frequently sacrifice pawns to open files and diagonals. They know that it will be possible to sacrifice pieces to destroy the pawn screen in front of their opponent's king, as the possibility of mate will justify the investment. This is easy to understand, but a pawn can often be sacrificed to open lines in the belief that the active piece play obtained will eventually lead to the investment's recovery with interest, despite the absence of a direct attack against the enemy king.

A good example of a whole opening system geared to this strategy is the Benko Gambit in which after 1 d4 Nf6 2 c4 c5 3 d5 Black sacrifices a pawn with 3 ... b5 4 cxb5 a6 5 bxa6 Bxa6. A possible continuation would then be 6 Nc3 d6 7 Nf3 g6 8 g3 Bg7 9 Bg2 0–0 10 0–0 Nbd7 (Diagram 29).

Black is a pawn down, but will develop pressure with rooks and queen on the a- and b-files in conjunction with pressure on the

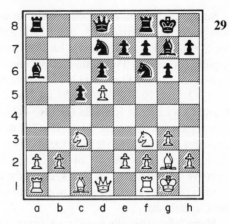

a1–h8 diagonal. Black will also develop pressure with his knights by establishing them on squares such as e5, a4, or d3 (after White's e-pawn has moved). Sacrifices on b2 are a frequent possibility, while on the other side of the coin White must hope to liquidate the pressure and remain a pawn up. Having said this it must be pointed out that simple liquidation of material will not solve White's problems as many endgames, especially major piece endings, will be better for Black due to the persisting bind and pressure on the Black squares of the a1–h8 diagonal.

A classic example of the power of play on half-open lines following a pawn sacrifice was given by Capablanca, with Black against Nimzowitsch at St. Petersburg, 1914 (see Diagram 30).

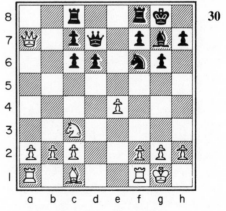

Nimzowitsch–Capablanca,
St. Petersburg, 1914

Superficially White is a safe pawn up with a superior pawn structure, but Black's play on the a- and b-files and a1–h8 diagonal is rapidly decisive. The game continued 14 Qa6 Rfe8 15 Qd3 Qe6 16 f3 Nd7 17 Bd2 Ne5 18 Qe2 Nc4 19 Rab1 Ra8 20 a4 Nxd2 21 Qxd2 Qc4 22 Rfd1 Reb8 23 Qe3 Rb4 (Black can regain his pawn by 23 ... Bxc3, but his pressure is worth more) 24 Qg5 Bd4+ 25 Kh1 Rab8 (the threat of 25 ... Bxc3 is decisive). White tried 26 Rxd4, but soon lost — a typically smooth and powerful display by Capablanca.

Hopefully, this discussion of open lines will give readers a taste of the most crucial positional principles and will help them to evaluate such lines, decide for or against their creation, and make decisions as regards which lines should be contested and which represent mere dead ends.

References

A. Kotov, *Think Like a Grandmaster.*
A. Kotov, *Play Like a Grandmaster.*
M. Stean, *Simple Chess.*
A. Nimzowitsch, *My System.*
R. Keene, *Nimzowitsch: A Reappraisal.*
D. Bronstein, *The Chess Struggle In Practice (Zurich 1953).*

Lessons 13–16

OPENING PRINCIPLES AND IDEAS

NIGEL DAVIES, I.M.

There have been thousands of books devoted to the opening. The poor reader is often encouraged to memorize hundreds of variations only to be discouraged and dismayed when results show no sign of improvement. Clearly an alternative approach is required.

These four lessons attempt to clarify the problems of the openings. The first three analyse games illustrating the elements (centre, development and planning) of the opening. In the fourth I will present some ideas which I hope will guide the reader towards better opening play.

LESSON 13. THE CENTRE

The centre of the chessboard is generally understood to be the squares d4, d5, e4 and e5. The importance of these squares can be illustrated by the following two diagrams.

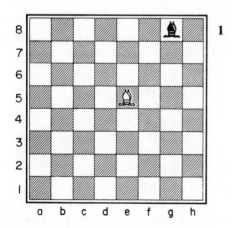

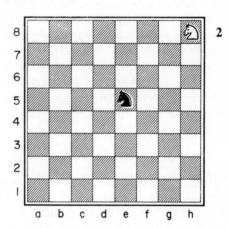

A comparison of the number of squares controlled by each piece shows that *centralized* pieces have far more *power*. It follows naturally that control of the centre is of great importance, and all good openings aim at control of these squares.

At one time direct occupation of the centre with pawns was considered the ideal. A pawn centre, when well supported with pieces, can certainly be a very powerful force, with a subsequent advance of the pawns driving the enemy pieces to poor (decentralized) squares.

However, modern players also appreciate an alternative philosophy; pressure on the centre with pieces.

These two ideas come into conflict in many modern opening variations, one of which is the Grünfeld Defence, Exchange Variation.

Amongst the many advocates of White's pawn centre is the young Soviet star Garry Kasparov.

Karparov–Natis, Malta Olympiad 1980

1 d4	Nf6
2 c4	g6
3 Nc3	d5
4 cxd5	Nxd5
5 e4	Nxc3
6 bxc3	Bg7
7 Nf3	c5

After seven moves, White has achieved the classical "ideal" of pawns on d4 and e4. By advancing these pawns further he aims to send the enemy forces into retreat and thus create a large "power differential" between the white and black armies. This "power differential" gives White attacking chances. On this occasion the attack continues into the endgame.

8 Rb1

Black's strategic aim is pressure against White's centre, making use of his fianchettoed bishop on the a1–h8 diagonal and moves such as ... c5, ... Nc6, and ... Bg4.

To counteract this pressure White often removes his rook from a1 so as to make the advance d4–d5 feasible. Recently the most popular way of doing this has been 8 Be3 and 9 Rb1, a sequence illustrated in the next game. Kasparov's last move, 8 Rb1, is as yet, relatively unexplored.

8 ...	0–0
9 Be2	Nc6

Also possible is 9 ... Qa5, though 10 Rb5 Qxc3+ 11 Bd2 Qa3 12 Rxc5 Qxa2 13 0–0 gives White a powerfully centralized army for his sacrificed pawn.

10 d5!	Bxc3+
11 Bd2	Bxd2+
12 Qxd2	Nd4

An interesting crossroads. After 12 ... Nb8, Black would keep his ill-gotten booty at the expense of a big "power differential". White would obtain dangerous attacking chances with 13 h4! Instead of this Black opts for the "safety" of an endgame, though

here too White's central control is a significant factor.

13 Nxd4	cxd4
14 Qxd4	Qa5+
15 Qd2	Qxd2+
16 Kxd2	Rd8
17 Ke3	b6
18 Rbc1 (see Diagram)	

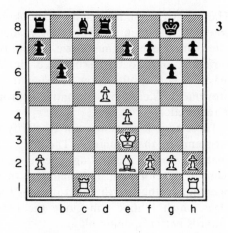

18 ...	e6
19 Bc4	e5

Also after 19 ... Kf8 20 Rhd1 Ke7 21 e5! White's central control leaves Black struggling.

20 Bb3	Bd7
21 Rc7	a5
22 d6	b5?

After this Black's resistance crumbles. He must prevent 23 f4 with 22 ... g5, when 23 g3 is met by 23 ... g4.

23 f4!	exf4+
24 Kxf4	Ra6
25 e5	a4
26 Bd5	a3
27 Rf1	Ra4+
28 Ke3	Be6
29 Bxe6	fxe6
30 Rff7	Rh4
31 Rg7+	Kh8
32 Rge7	**Black resigned**.

The Grünfeld Defence has been "refuted" and rehabilitated many times since its introduction by the Austrian grandmaster Ernst Grünfeld in Vienna in 1922.

In the next game White plays the latest "refutation" and one which has caused Black a lot of trouble recently. By bolstering d4 (8 Be3) and removing his rook from the a1–h8 diagonal (9 Rc1) he aims to neutralize Black's fianchettoed bishop. The theory goes that Black will then be unable to generate sufficient central counterplay and get squashed by White's centre pawns.

However, there are Grünfeld experts who continue to believe in the pent-up energy in Black's set-up and search diligently for new methods of counterplay. Numbered among these players are Grandmasters Timman, Ftacnik, Smejkal, Jansa, Sax, Uhlmann, Adorjan . . . and Shamkovich.

Fedorowicz–Shamkovich, New York 1980

1	d4	Nf6
2	Nf3	g6
3	c4	Bg7
4	Nc3	d5
5	cxd5	Nxd5
6	e4	Nxc3
7	bxc3	c5
8	Be3	Bg4
9	Rc1	Qa5
10	Qd2	Bxf3
11	gxf3	Nd7
12	d5	b5!

White has obtained the bishop pair and occupied the centre with pawns. In spite of this a closer inspection shows that matters are not easy for him. Black's last five moves form a sequence specially designed to disrupt the natural rhythm of White's development. With 10 ... Bxf3 he inflicted a gash in White's pawn structure making it difficult for the white monarch to find a safe home. His last move (12 ... b5!) discourages White from supporting his centre with 13 c4, as the reply 13 ... b4 would threaten 14 ... Bc3.

Over the next few moves Black makes a fierce attack on White's centre and the balance of power tilts in his favour.

13	f4	Rd8!
14	c4	b4
15	e5	g5!
16	Bh3	e6!
17	Rg1	

A rather flimsy attempt to support his collapsing centre. 17 dxe6 Nxe5! would also be good for Black.

17	...	gxf4
18	Rxg7	Nxe5!
19	Ke2	fxe3
20	Qb2	

Black's next move destroys the last remnants of White's centre and signals the start of a new phase. After the brilliant marshalling of his forces in the opening, Shamkovich switches to a direct attack on White's king (see Diagram).

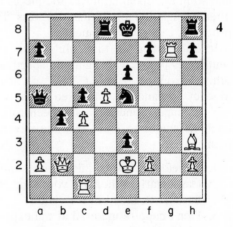

20	...	Rxd5!!

Now it is Black's pieces that occupy the centre!

21	cxd5	Qa6+
22	Kxe3	Qd3+
23	Kf4	f6

Threatening mate with 24 ... Qf3.

| 24 | Qb3 | |

Alternatives are no better. Both 24 Rg3 Ng6+ 25 Rxg6 e5+ and 24 Bg2 Ng6+ 25 Rxg6 e5+ 26 Kg4 Qxg6+ lead to mate.

	24 ...	Ng6+
	25 Rxg6	

After 25 Kg4 h5 White is checkmated.

	25 ...	e5+
	26 Kg4	h5+
	27 Kh4	Qe4+

White resigned.

Both 28 Kg3 h4 and 28 Bg4 hxg4+ 29 Kg3 Rh3 are mate.

LESSON 14. DEVELOPMENT

In the initial position, both Black and White have their pieces poorly placed at the edge of the board. It is very logical for them both to want to improve this state of affairs and so in the opening moves the pieces are often brought to more influential posts. This process is called development.

It often happens that whilst one side centralizes pieces with lightning speed, the other develops without any particular urgency . . . and gets murdered. To prevent such carnage, principles have been formulated as guides to good opening development:

1. Develop pieces as quickly as possible.
2. Castle early, otherwise your king may become stranded in the centre.
3. Don't capture material at the expense of development.
4. Don't move the same piece twice.
5. Don't move the queen out too early. The queen will be forced into making time-wasting retreats if attacked by pieces of lesser value.
6. Don't make too many pawn moves at the expense of developing the pieces.

These principles find illustration in the following games:

Davies–Baljon, London 1980 (Sicilian Defence)

1	e4	c5
2	Nf3	d6
3	Bb5+	Nd7
4	d4	Nf6
5	0–0!?	

An interesting gambit which started to appear in a few games when it was discovered that 5 Nc3 cxd4 6 Qxd4 e5! 7 Qd3 h6! (preventing 8 Bg5) gave White nothing. Now after 5 ... cxd4 6 Qxd4 e5 7 Qd3 h6, White can play 8 c4! with a bind.

	5 ...	Nxe4

Snatching a pawn at the expense of development. Despite the risks involved, such a pawn snatch is sometimes possible. In the razor-sharp Sicilian Najdorf, Poisoned Pawn Variation (1 e4 c5 2 Nf3 d6 3 d4 cxd4 4 Nxd4 Nf6 5 Nc3 a6 6 Bg5 e6 7 f4 Qb6 8 Qd2 Qxb2) Black's pawn-snatch is justified by the damage thereby inflicted on White's queen-side. Here, the pawn captured is an important central pawn.

	6 Qe2	Nf6

The price of the pawn. Black has had to move this knight three times (4 ... Nf6, 5 ... Nxe4 and 6 ... Nf6).

7	dxc5	dxc5
8	Rd1	e6
9	Bg5	h6
10	Bh4	Qb6?

A violation of principle. Black frees himself from the pin on the d-file and the h4–d8 diagonal, but in doing so moves the queen out too early — leaving the king-side undeveloped and the king uncastled.

Instead, he should play the calm 10 ... Be7!!, when White's attempt to win a piece with 11 Ne5 rebounds after 11 ... 0–0! (castle early!) 12 Bxf6 Bxf6 13 Bxd7 Bxe5 14 Bxc8? Qf6 and Black wins. Or 13 Nxd7 Bxd7 14 Rxd7 Qc8 with threats of Bxb2 and a6. White, in turn, should not move a piece twice with 11 Ne5, but concentrate on quick development with 11 Nc3.

11 Na3

Threatening to win time on Black's prematurely developed queen, with 12 Nc4 (12 ... Qxb5 13 Nd6+).

11 ...	a6
12 Bxd7+	Bxd7
13 Nc4	Qa7

After 13 ... Qc7, 14 Bg3 is very unpleasant for Black.

14 Nce5 (see diagram)

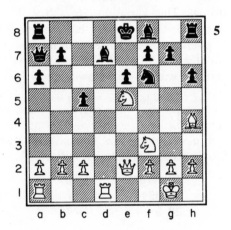

14 ...   Bc8

A retrograde step, although, as the following variations show, the power differential between White's centralized army and Black's scattered rabble had already become too great.

(a) 14 ... Rd8 15 Nxf7! Kxf7 16 Ne5+ Kg8 (if 16 ... Ke7 then 17 Ng6+ and 18 Nxh8, or if 16 ... Ke8 then 17 Bxf6 gxf6 18 Qh5+ Ke7 19 Qf7 is mate) 17 Bxf6 gxf6 18 Qg4+ Bg7 19 Rxd7 Rxd7 20 Qxe6+ and 21 Nxd7 wins.

(b) 14 ... Bc6 15 Nxf7!! Kxf7 (15 ... Bxf3 16 Qxf3 Kxf7 17 Rd7+ and 18 Rxb7 wins Black's queen) 16 Ne5+ Kg8 17 Bxf6 gxf6 18 Qg4+ Bg7 19 Qxe6+ Kh7 20 Nxc6 bxc6 21 Rd7 and now:

(i) 21 ... Qb6 22 Qf5+ Kg8 23 Rad1

(threatening 24 Rxg7+) 23 ... Rf8 (if 23 ... Rh7 then 24 Qe6+ Kh8 25 Qe7 gives the deadly threat of 26 Rd8 — or if 23 ... Ra7, then 24 Rxa7 Qxa7 25 Rd8+ Bf8 26 Rd7) 24 Rxg7+ Kxg7 25 Qg4+ with mate to follow.

(ii) 21 ... Qb8 22 Qf5+ Kg8 23 Rad1 (threatening 24 Rxg7+) 23 ... Qf8 (if 23 ... Qe8, then 24 Rxg7+ Kxg7 25 Rd7+ winning, if 23 ... Qe5 24 Qg6, or if 23 ... Rh7 then 24 Qe6+ Kh8 25 Qe7 Qg8 26 Rd8 Bf8 27 Qxf6+ wins) 24 Qe6+ Kh7 25 Rf7 Qe8 26 Rxg7+ Kxg7 27 Rd7+ Qxd7 28 Qxd7+ and Black has too many weak pawns to put up much resistance in the endgame.

After 14 ... Bc8, the win is simpler . . .

15 Nxf7!!	Kxf7
16 Ne5+	Kg8

After 16 ... Ke8, there is the beautiful finish 17 Qh5+ Nxh5 18 Rd8 mate, whilst 16 ... Ke7 simply allows 17 Qh5 and 18 Qf7 mate.

17 Bxf6	b5

Or 17 ... gxf6 18 Qg4+ Bg7 19 Rd8 mate.

18 Qg4	Qc7
19 Rd8	h5
20 Qg5	Rh6
21 Rxf8+	Kxf8
22 Bxg7+	Qxg7
23 Qd8 mate.	

The next game shows that on a bad day even grandmasters can neglect development, with equally disastrous consequences.

Andersson–Portisch (Skopje Olympiad, 1972) (Sicilian Defence)

1 e4	c5
2 Nf3	d6
3 Bb5+	Nc6
4 0–0	Bd7
5 Re1	Nf6
6 c3	a6
7 Bf1	

At this point, White can offer an interesting gambit with 7 Bxc6 Bxc6 8 d4, though the careful text move is more in keeping with Andersson's style. White appears to be retreating but his pieces occupy posts which will be very effective in the approaching middle game. Very effective development.

| 7 ... | e5 |
| 8 h3 | |

An important precaution which is also seen in the Ruy Lopez (1 e4 e5 2 Nf3 Nc6 3 Bb5 a6 4 Ba4 Nf6 5 0–0 Be7 6 Re1 b5 7 Bb3 d6 8 c3 0–0 9 h3). The immediate 8 d4 would allow 8 ... cxd4 9 cxd4 Bg4 with counterplay.

| 8 ... | h6?! |

This, on the other hand, is merely a waste of time. 8 ... Be7 9 d4 Qc7 would have been better, when Black has a solid position

| 9 d4 | Qc7 |
| 10 a4 | g6? |

Instead of the normal 10 ... Be7, Portisch produces a move which not only wastes time but also weakens the squares d6 and c5. As a result the black king gets caught in the centre.

11 Na3	Bg7
12 dxc5	dxc5
13 Nc4	

. . . and Black is in trouble.

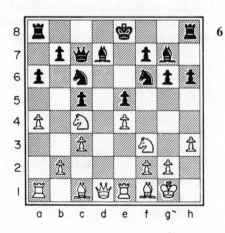

White threatens to win a pawn with 14 Qd6 and 13 ... 0–0 doesn't help after 14 Qd6! Qxd6 15 Nxd6 Rab8 16 Be3 — or if 15 ... b6 16 Nc4!

| 13 ... | Rb8 |
| 14 b4! | |

The immediate 14 Nd6+ would allow the calm reply 14 ... Ke7. After 14 b4! the threat is 15 b5!

| 14 ... | cxb4 |
| 15 cxb4 | Be6 |

If 15 ... Nxb4 then 16 N(c4)xe5!, threatening both 17 Bf4 and 17 Qb3, is terribly strong. The variation 16 ... Nc2 17 Bf4 Nxe1 18 Qxe1 would have seen White recovering the exchange with interest.

After 15 ... 0–0 White would have won material with 16 b5 followed by 17 Ba3.

| 16 Nd6+ | Ke7 |
| 17 Ba3 | Ne8 |

The variation 17 ... Qxd6 18 b5 Nb4 19 Qxd6+ is also hopeless for Black.

18 Nxb7!	Qxb7
19 b5+	Kf6
20 bxc6	Qc7

Or if 20 ... Qxc6 21 Nxe5! Kxe5 22 f4+ Kxf4 (22 ... Kf6 23 Qd4 mate) 23 e5 (or 23 Qf3+ etc.) wins.

| 21 Nxe5! | (1–0) |

Neither 21 ... Qxe5 22 Qf3+ Bf5 23 exf5 Qxf5 24 Be7 mate nor 21 ... Kxe5 22 f4+ Kxf4 23 e5 must have seemed attractive possibilities.

LESSON 15. PLANNING

It often happens that a player develops pieces quickly and plays for the centre, but is suddenly at a complete loss as to what to do. These developed, centralized forces suddenly look quite ineffective and the advent of the middlegame sees the position drifting slowly but irrevocably downhill.

The reason for eventual defeat is that the opening has been played superficially, without bearing in mind the subsequent middlegame. The lesson to be learned is that even in the opening the strategic features of a position must be recognized and the pieces developed on appropriate squares. The opening must be played according to a plan.

The contrast between the following two games is very instructive.

Capablanca–Janowsky, St. Petersburg 1914

1 e4	e5
2 Nf3	Nc6
3 Bb5	a6
4 Bxc6	dxc6
5 Nc3	Bc5

Janowsky puts the bishop on its "most aggressive" square. 6 Nxe5 would not be answered by 6 ... Bxf2+ 7 Kxf2 Qd4+ 8 Ke1 Qxe5 9 d4 but instead by 6 ... Qd4 7 Nd3 Ba7 when White is rather tied up.

| 6 d3 | Bg4 |

And now the other bishop takes up an aggressive position.

7 Be3	Bxe3
8 fxe3	Qe7
9 0-0	0-0-0
10 Qe1	Nh6

It seems that Black's moves have followed all the rules. He has developed quickly, brought his king to safety and shown a regard for the centre, yet from now on his position slowly but surely deteriorates.

The truth of the matter is that Black has played the opening planlessly. He has surrendered his major trump, the bishop pair (7 ... Bxe3) and in doing so strengthened White's grip on the centre (8 fxe3). Not only does Black no longer have access to d4 but he has also presented White with the half-open f-file.

From here Capablanca's play is an object lesson in methodical, clear-headed strategy, demolishing Janowsky's king-position

square by square. Further commentary seems superfluous.

11 Rb1! f6 12 b4 Nf7 13 a4 Bxf3 14 Rxf3 b6 15 b5! (see diagram)

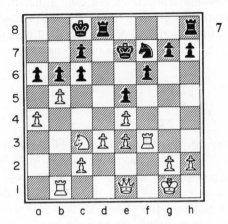

15 ... cxb5 16 axb5 a5 17 Nd5! Qc5 18 c4 Ng5 19 Rf2 Ne6 20 Qc3 Rd7 21 Rd1 Kb7 22 d4 Qd6 23 Rc2 exd4 24 exd4 Nf4 25 c5! Nxd5 26 exd5 Qxd5 27 c6+ Kb8 28 cxd7 Qxd7 29 d5 Re8 30 d6 cxd6 31 Qc6 and White won.

Romanovsky–Botvinnik, Moscow 1935

1 e4	e5
2 Nf3	Nc6
3 Bb5	a6
4 Bxc6	dxc6
5 Nc3	f6!
6 d3	

At one time White played this variation with a view to obtaining a qualitatively superior pawn majority on the king-side after 6 d4 exd4 7 Qxd4 Qxd4 8 Nxd4. Practice has since shown that Black's pair of bishops provide excellent compensation for his inferior pawns and White has virtually abandoned this line of play.

Romanovsky's idea is different. By keeping the position closed he seeks to restrict the activity of Black's bishop pair. Eventually, and according to circumstance, he plans a breakthrough with f4 or d4.

Botvinnik's play makes a fascinating contrast with that of Janowsky in the previous example. First of all he sets up a central bastion (5 ... f6! and 7 ... c5!) and then by the harmonious placement of his pieces prevents White from realizing either of his strategic objectives (d4 or f4). He then goes on to prepare and play ... f5, the first stage in the liberation of his bishop pair.

6 ...	Bd6
7 Be3	c5!
8 Ne2	Ne7
9 Ng3	

The advance f4 turns out to be difficult to organize. A game Tartakover–Alekhine, Semmering 1926, continued: 9 Nd2 Ng6 10 0–0 0–0 11 Nb3 b6 12 Kh1 Qe7 13 f4 when 13 ... f5! 14 fxe5 Nxe5 15 exf5 Ng4 would have given Black the better game.

9 ...	Be6
10 c3	Qd7
11 0–0	0–0
12 Qc2	

After 12 d4 Black could play 12 ... cxd4 13 cxd4 exd4 14 Nxd4 Bc4 with good play.

12 ...	Nc6
13 Nd2	Rad8
14 Rad1	b6
15 f3	

Pushing this pawn one square further would have been disastrous after 15 ... exf4 16 Bxf4 Bxf4 17 Rxf4 Ne5!

15 ...	Be7
16 Nb3	a5
17 Nc1	Bd6
18 Qf2	Ne7
19 Rd2	f5!

In his excellent book *One Hundred Selected Games* Botvinnik states:

"It is useful now to make certain deductions with regard to the opening system White has chosen. White's basic idea (the break-through at d4 and f4) has not been realized. In the future also

White is continually forced to pursue waiting tactics.

Black has the initiative, but it is not easy for him to find a sound plan."

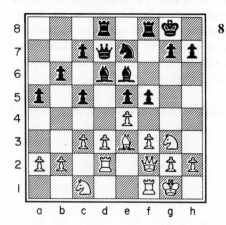

"Black's move 19 looks rather risky, as the e-pawn is weakened and White gets e4. But in reality Black can avoid the weakness at e5 (by transferring the knight to f4, where White will have to exchange it) while the e4 square is far from Black's camp, and its occupation by White is more than offset by the opening of the f-file and Black's freer position" (Botvinnik).

There now followed a complicated struggle in which Botvinnik finally managed to direct his pair of bishops at the enemy king. Strictly speaking the rest of the game falls outside my province, though I include it to show the eventual triumph of Botvinnik's masterful strategy:

20 exf5 Nxf5 21 Ne4 h6 22 Qe1 Be7 23 Bf2 Bd5 24 Qe2 Rfe8 25 Rdd1 Qe6 26 Rfe1 Bf8 27 Qc2 Qf7 28 Rd2 Re6 29 Rde2 Rde8 30 Qa4 Ne7 31 Bg3 Bc6 32 Qc2 Nd5 33 Nb3 g5 34 Nbd2 Bg7 35 Nf1 R6e7 36 Rd2 Rd7 37 Ne3 Nxe3 38 Rxe3 Qxa2 39 h4 gxh4 40 Bxh4 Qf7 41 Rde2 Rf8 42 Bg3 Qg6 43 Kf2 h5 44 Nd2 Bh6 45 Rxe5 Rg7 46 Nf1 h4 47 Bxh4 Bxf3! 48 Kg1 Bxe2 49 Rxe2 Qh5 50 Re4 Rf4 51 Rxf4 Bxf4 52 Qb3+ Kh7 53 Bf2 Qf3 54 g3 Qxd3 55 Qe6 Bh6 56 Qh3 Rf7 57 Ne3 Qb1+ 58 Nf1 Qf5 59 Qh2 a4 White resigned.

LESSON 16. IDEAS FOR
AN OPENING REPERTOIRE

With the completion of Lesson 15 my discussion of principles has come to an end. With the correct application of these principles, excellent opening play will result, although rather than always working from first principles a formula can be applied and used as a short cut. This magic formula is called on opening repertoire.

Developing an opening repertoire can be likened to the purchase of a new suit. Ideally it should be tailor-made for you and fit your style of play perfectly. Unfortunately chess tailors are a rare commodity outside the Soviet Union, so you must do your own work.

The first, and perhaps most difficult, stage in the process is to choose your openings. A player with flair for attack should play openings which seize the initiative even at the cost of positional or material concessions, whilst those with a penchant for long-term strategy should adopt a more solid approach.

In your choice you should bear in mind the practical consideration of time. Most amateurs have little time available for chess and should therefore think twice before adopting sharp, highly analysed variations which require months of detailed work.

Instead I recommend the adoption of less fashionable openings which, not being under constant theoretical review, have fewer variations and so need less study. The following openings are all interesting possibilities.

Veresov Opening (1 d4 Nf6 2 Nc3 d5 3 Bg5)

A good method of opening a chess game, the Veresov can be interpreted in either a solid or a sharp manner. Its recent and successful adoption by Britain's Tony Miles is just one testimony to its value.

Typical play occurs in the variation 1 d4 Nf6 2 Nc3 d5 3 Bg5 Nbd7 4 Nf3 g6 5 e3 Bg7 6 Bd3 0–0 7 0–0 c5 8 Re1 b6 9 e4 when White has pressure.

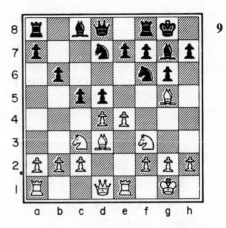

9

Chigorin Defence (1 d4 d5 2 c4 Nc6)

Invented last century by the great Russian master Mikhail Ivanovich Chigorin, this defence is the spiritual ancestor of the Nimzo–Indian and Grünfeld Defences. Both Smyslov and Bronstein have been attracted by the chances it offers for lively piece play.

Some of Black's chances are illustrated by the variation 1 d4 d5 2 c4 Nc6 3 Nf3 Bg4 4 cxd5 Bxf3 5 gxf3 Qxd5 6 e3 e5 7 Nc3 Bb4 8 Bd2 Bxc3 9 bxc3 Qd6. White has a strong centre and pair of bishops, but his king will have trouble finding safety from the active black pieces.

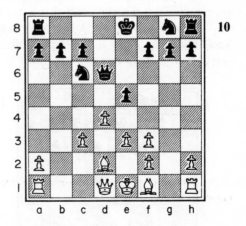

10

Centre Counter Defence (1 e4 d5)

Despite the loss of time involved after 2 exd5 Qxd5 3 Nc3 Qa5, Black can achieve a solid set-up. Having been adopted by grand-masters such as Bronstein and Lein, it certainly deserves to be taken seriously.

Black's position develops harmoniously in the variation 1 e4 d5 2 exd5 Qxd5 3 Nc3 Qa5 4 d4 c6 5 Nf3 Bg4 6 Bc4 Nf6 7 h3 (7 Bxf7+? Kxf7 8 Ne5+ Qxe5+) 7 ... Bxf3 8 Qxf3 e6.

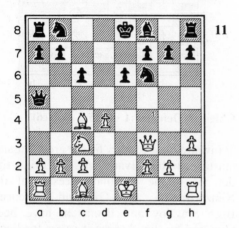

Albin Counter Gambit (1 d4 d5 2 c4 e5 3 dxe5 d4)

This opening will certainly appeal to chess d'Artagnans. Black gains space in the centre, castles long and launches a direct attack on the unsuspecting white monarch.

An example of play is the game Levitt–Speelman, Torquay 1982, which went 1 d4 d5 2 c4 e5 3 dxe5 d4 4 Nf3 Nc6 5 g3 Be6 6 Nbd2 Qd7 7 a3 Nge7 8 Nb3 Ng6 9 Nbxd4 0–0–0 with a sharp and unclear position.

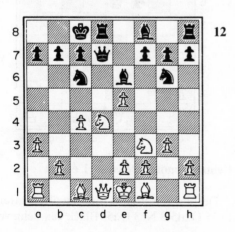

Sicilian Defence, Rossolimo Variation (1 e4 c5 2 Nf3 Nc6 3 Bb5)

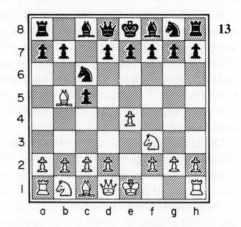

Along with its sister variation (1 e4 c5 2 Nf3 d6 3 Bb5+) I can warmly recommend this method of fighting the Sicilian. It can be interpreted in either positional or gambit style, the games in Lesson 14 illustrating both these facets.

Ruy Lopez, Delayed Exchange Variation (1 e4 e5 2 Nf3 Nc6 3 Bb5 a6 4 Ba4 Nf6 5 Bxc6 dxc6)

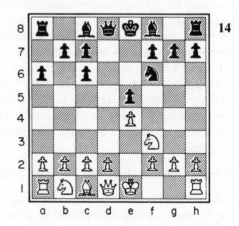

The Delayed Exchange Variation is an excellent choice for solid strategists. A more refined version occurs after 1 e4 e5 2 Nf3 Nc6 3 Bb5 a6 4 Ba4 Nf6 5 0–0 Be7 6 Bxc6 when Black's bishop has been prematurely committed to e7.

Having decided upon a repertoire, the next stage is to acquire an extensive knowledge and understanding of your chosen systems. Repeating them in both serious and "friendly" games will contribute towards this though I would like to recommend a more serious approach. My own method is to annotate and file both my own games and any master games that occur within my repertoire. Once this becomes a routine it takes up surprisingly little time and can pay rich dividends.

Finally I should like to say a few words about the purchase of books on openings. Volumes such as *Modern Chess Openings* and *Encyclopaedia of Chess Openings* can give a useful overview though books cover-ing just one variation are a different kettle of fish entirely.

The authors of such books may or may not be experts in the variation they have written about. If they aren't then they will have little of interest to say whilst if they are, they probably won't want to say it.

My advice is to follow the example of masters and grandmasters who generally limit their acquisitions to a selection of *Chess Informants* (particularly important), magazines, and tournament bulletins. By filing the appropriate games from such sources you will have access to a more personal, comprehensive and up-to-date source of reference than any chess book could offer.

Lessons 17–20

ENDINGS

IAN D. MULLEN

The four lessons which follow give a gentle introduction to the ending. This is traditionally the part of the game that club players are loath to reach and loathe even more to study. It follows that this is the part of the game where they are often at their weakest.

The lessons have been arranged under the headings of king and pawn; minor piece; rook and pawn; and queen and pawn endings. The section on rook and pawn spills over two lessons in order to keep an even balance in length.

The endings are to chess as putting is to golf. Love them or loathe them, if your aim is to be a strong player you must learn them!

LESSON 17. KING AND PAWN ENDINGS

King and pawn endings occur only rarely in practical play, but are fundamental to the game in every sense. One good reason for their relative non-appearance is the fact that all but the more complex positions will be evaluated easily by the technically well-equipped player; and mutual respect will preclude playing on in a clearly won, drawn, or lost position. *One pawn down in an otherwise equal king and pawn ending will generally soon crystallize into a queen down!* — a point which is not appreciated fully by many amateurs, who may feel that they are doing well to reach such a situation.

It would seem obvious that these endings, being the most simplified, would also be the easiest to play. To a certain extent this is true; but behind the scenes are a whole wealth of subtle *ideas* and *techniques*. A thorough study of the following pages should equip the student with knowledge enough to master most of the positions likely to arise in over-the-board play. Also, and perhaps more important, the student might then be able to assess the pawn situation in any position more clearly and have a greater understanding of the positional and tactical themes related to pawn play in general.

"Pawns are the soul of chess", but we will start with the bare bones:

King vs. King, the Opposition

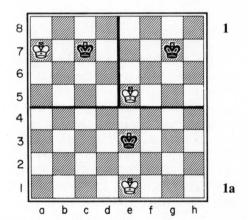

The kings are said to be in opposition when they are separated by only one square either vertically, horizontally, or diagonally. In such a situation the side whose turn it is to move is generally at a *disadvantage* as ground must be conceded. The other side is then said to hold the OPPOSITION. In Diagram 1a the outcome depends on the move. White to play cannot progress past the first

rank as long as Black maintains the opposition, e.g. 1 Kd1 Kd3 2 Kc1 Kc3, etc.
Black to move must relinquish the opposition and is powerless to prevent White's
king from reaching the eighth rank (e.g.
1 ... Kd3 2 Kf2 Ke4 3 Kg3 — or Ke2
regaining the opposition — Kf5 4 Kh4 Kg6 5
Kg4 etc.). This compulsion to concede
ground by being forced to move (zugzwang)
is often a decisive factor in very simplified
positions.

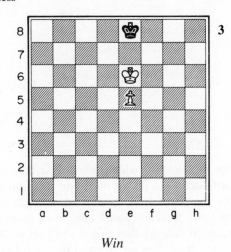

Win

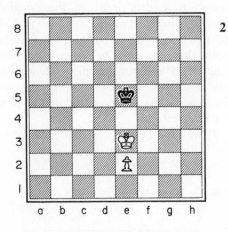

Win or Draw

In Diagram 3 White wins *whoever moves*.
   (a) 1 ... Kf8 2 Kd7, then 3 e6, 4 e7, 5 e8
(Q) . . .
   (b) 1 Kf6 Kf8 2 e6 Ke8 3 e7 Kd7 4 Kf7
+−. Similarly with 1 Kd6. This holds good
also for king plus queen pawn, bishop pawn
or knight pawn. The only exception to
Diagrams 2 and 3 occurs in the well-known
king plus rook pawn *vs.* king ending, which
is drawn if the defending side can *blockade*
the pawn (Diagram 4a), or *confine* the white
king in front of the pawn (Diagram 4b).

Viz., in this important position White to
move *draws*, Black to move *loses*. With
White to play, Black simply maintains the
opposition. To make progress White then
has to advance the pawn *ahead* of the king
and can only achieve *stalemate*, e.g. 1 Kf3
Kf5! 2 e4+ Ke5 3 Ke3 Ke6! 4 Kd4 Kd6! 5
e5+ Ke6 6 Ke4 Ke7! 7 Kf5 Kf7! 8 e6+ Ke7 9
Ke5 Ke8! 10 Kf6 Kf8 11 e7+ Ke8 12 Ke6
Stalemate. Black to move must concede
ground and White advances the king to clear
a path for the pawn to queen, e.g. 1 ... Kf5
2 Kd4! Ke6 3 Ke4!! (White's king must stay
ahead of the pawn- e3?, e4? =) Kf6 4 Kd5!
Kf5 5 e4+ Kf6 6 Kd6 (*building a bridge*) Kf7
7 e5 Ke8 8 Ke6! +− (see Diagram 3, White
now wins whoever moves). Diagram 2 is one
position which should be *fully mastered*
[*N.B. White aims to keep the king ahead on
the sixth rank.*]

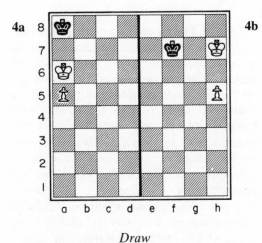

Draw

Diagram 4a leads to stalemate (1 Kb6 Kb8 2
a6 Ka8 3 a7=). In Diagram 4b White has the
choice of stalemating Black (1 h6 Kf8 2 Kg6

as before) or inflicting a self-stalemate! (1 Kh8 Kf8 2 h6 Kf7 3 h7 Kf8=). The point to notice is that if the defending side can reach a corner square or else f7, f8 (in Diagram 4b; c7, c8 in Diagram 4a etc.), it is a DRAW. A full understanding of these "simple" king plus pawn endings is really the key to all that follows in this section.

Examples of Opposition

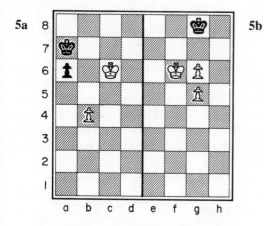

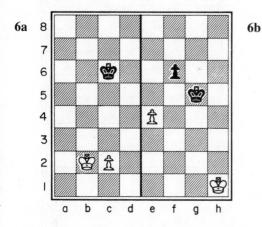

Diagram 5a is drawn. White to play can win the pawn, but Black gains the opposition through a clever tactic. 1 Kc7 Ka8 2 Kb6 a5! 3 Kxa5 (3 bxa5 leaves king plus rook pawn vs. king =) 3 ... Ka7 = as Black holds the opposition.

In example 5b White has only to be wary of *stalemate* in order to win easily: 1 g7 Kh7 2 g8(Q)+! Kxg8 3 Kg6! +−.

The distant opposition occurs when the kings are opposing with three or sometimes five squares between them.

Often what looks like witchcraft here is solely a matter of *technique*. In Diagram 6a Black has a choice of no less than *seven* losing moves and only one which draws. Black must seize the distant opposition, thus: 1 ... Kb6!!(=). On 2 Kb3 Kb5 or 2 Kc3 Kc5.

Note that on 1 ... Kb5? 2 Kb3 +−, 1 ... Kc5? 2 Kc3 +−, or 1 ... Kd5? 2 Kb3 +− (diagonal opposition).

Position 6b looks hopeless for White, but there is a superb defence available. 1 e5!! fxe5 2 Kg1!!(=) — the point is that White is now *ready to seize the direct opposition* and thus draw.

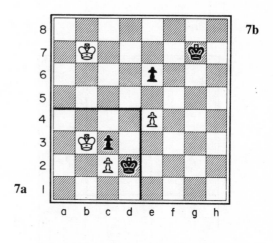

Pawn on 5th vs. pawn on 6th

In position 7a whoever moves loses! Bear this in mind for Diagram 7b where White can win by 1 e5! Kg6 2 Kc6 Kg5 3 Kd7! (3 Kd6?? loses!) Kf5 4 Kd6 +−. A delicate dance.

If White allows the defence 1 ... e5! then Black will draw by answering Kxe5 with ... Ke7, taking the opposition.

Tempo moves (Spare pawn moves)

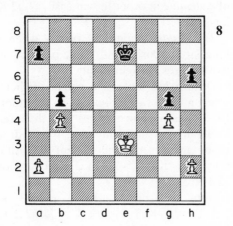

This position would be drawn were it not for the fact that White has more spare pawn moves available and can thus take the opposition: 1 Ke4 Ke6 2 a3 a6 3 h3! +−. Notice that it would be drawn if Black's h-pawn were unmoved!

The "Square"

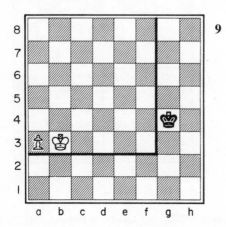

The heavy line shows the imaginary "square of the pawn". The horizontal length is the same as the distance between the pawn and its queening square. White to move plays 1 a4 and promotes unhindered as Black is *outside the square*. Black to play enters the square with 1 ... Kf5 2 Kc4 Ke6 3 Kc5 Kd7 4 Kb6 Kc8 (the vital square, compare Diagram 4b) and *draws*.

Einstein's King

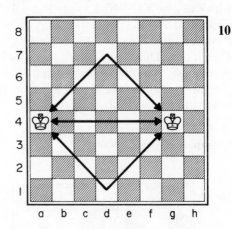

Idea. The task is to move White's king from a4 to g4. Geometrical principles do not hold! The king is as quick going via d7 as in a straight line. This gives rise to some brilliant ideas involving the king's capacity to operate in two directions simultaneously, e.g.:

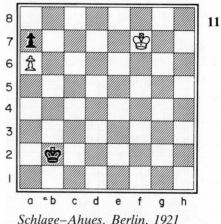

Schlage–Ahues, Berlin, 1921

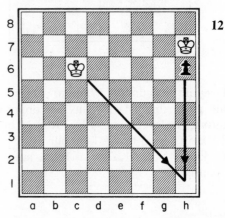

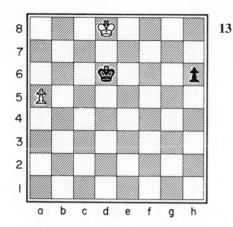

13

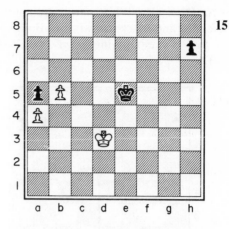

15

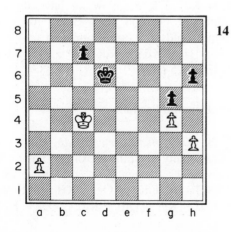

14

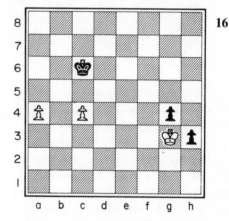

16

11. *Technique*. White can win by simultaneously approaching the pawn and heading off the black king, i.e. 1 Ke6! Kc3! 2 Kd5!! +− (in the game White actually played 2 Kd6? and Black drew as his king reaches c7 via 2 ... Kd4!!).

12. *Optical illusion*. Black to move. Which king is nearer the black pawn . . . ?

. . . Obviously the one on c6, as it is within the square of the pawn.

13. $E=MC^2$. Based on a famous idea by Reti. White seems hopelessly placed but manages to draw by threatening to queen. 1 Kc8 Kc6 2 Kb8! Kb5 3 Kb7! Kxa5 4 Kc6!(=) as White has miraculously entered the square of the pawn.

Positional Themes

14. *The Distant Passed Pawn* (D.P.P.) wins. Other things being equal, this is a *big positional advantage* in a pawn ending. 1 a4, and it can be seen that Black's king must leave the centre to stop the D.P.P. White then exchanges the a-pawn for Black's c-pawn and mops up the king-side pawns with a better-placed king. Try it out and see! This is one idea which is of *immense use in practical play* and helps to demonstrate the value of the oft-quoted "queen-side (distant) pawn-majority".

15. The *Protected Passed Pawn* (P.P.P.) wins. This is *stronger even than the D.P.P.* White wins very easily in the diagrammed position. The black king is tied to the square of the P.P.P. and can never capture the defending pawn. White's king is free to roam the board and can capture the h-pawn to win without difficulty.

16. *Draw*. The White pawns are mutually defended and Black has a P.P.P. Both kings are tied to the opposing pawns (1 ... Kc5 2 a5!).

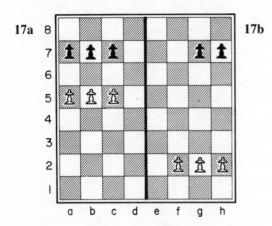

17(a). *Pawn breakthrough*. White can make a sacrificial breakthrough and queen before the black pawns get anywhere. 1 b6!! axb6 (1 ... cxb6 2 a6!) 2 c6! bxc6 3 a6 +−.

How does White create a passed pawn in Diagram 17(b) . . . ? The positionally correct move is 1 f4!, pushing the *candidate* (the one that will eventually be passed). 1 g4? would normally be a positional disaster. 1 ... g5!, and White's majority is temporarily crippled. The idea of one pawn holding two (or three) is both common and important.

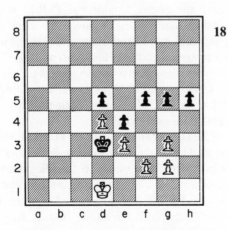

Müller–Svacina, Vienna 1941

Here is one of the most spectacular breakthroughs to have occurred in over-the-board play. White can draw by simple king moves, but is lured over a cliff by the scent of victory. 1 ... Kc4! (unashamedly playing for a trap) 2 Kc2 Kb5 3 Kb3 Kc6 4 Kb4 Kd6 5 Kb5 Kd7 6 Kc5 Ke6 7 Kc6? (7 Kb4 draws) 7 ... g4 8 Kc5 f4!! (the surprise) 9 exf4 (gxf4 h4) 9 ... h4! 10 gxh4 g3! 11 fxg3 e3 −+.

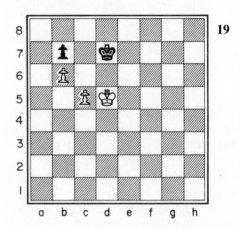

Triangulation. White must manoeuvre to gain the opposition and be wary of stalemate. This can be done by making use of the magic triangle in order to *lose* a move. The obvious does not work:

1 c6+? bxc6+? 2 Kc5 +−. (2 ... Kd8 3 Kd6!)

1 c6+? Kc8!(=) and on 2 c7 White has no more than stalemate. However, White moves in a *triangular* fashion and *loses* a move with 1 Ke5! Kc6 (1 ... Ke7 2 c6!) 2 Kd4 Kd7 3 Kd5!. Now we have the diagrammed position with Black to move. White holds the opposition and now wins easily (1 ... Kd8 2 Kd6 Kc8 3 Ke7 Kb8 4 Kd7 Ka8 5 c6 +−).

Problematic Positions

20. *King plus queen vs. king plus queen* occasionally wins; the proximity of the white king spells danger here. 1 f7 h2 2 f8(Q) h1(Q) 3 Qf3+ Kg1 4 Qe3+ Kf1 5 Qc1+ Kg2 6 Qd2+ Kf1 7 Qd1+ Kg2 8 Qe2+ Kg1 9

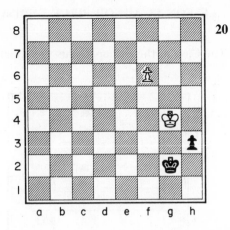

20

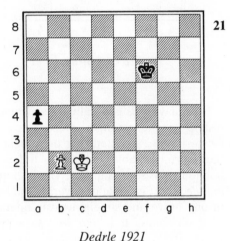

21

Dedrle 1921

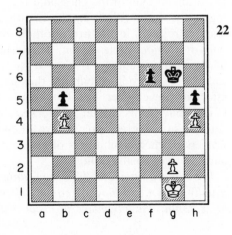

22

Botvinnik 1945

Kg3! +−. Black must surrender the queen to temporarily stave off mate.

21. *Reculer pour mieux sauter*. This is a position which would be fiendishly difficult to solve without an understanding of basic ideas. White must anticipate Black's threat of 1 ... a3!, which draws against all but 1 Kb1!! a3! 2 b3! (b4?=) 2 ... Ke5 3 Ka2 Kd5 4 Kxa3 Kc5 5 Ka4! +−. The point. White keeps the king *ahead* of the pawn and wins.

22. *Botvinnik's study*. The possibility of creating a D.P.P. wins for White even though the black king is well placed. 1 Kf2 Kf5 2 Kf3 Ke5 3 g4 hxg4+ 4 Kxg4 Ke4 5 h5 f5+ 6 Kh3! (the finesse, 6 Kg3 allows Black to advance *with check*.) 6 ... f4 7 h6 f3 8 h7 f2 9 Kg2! +−.

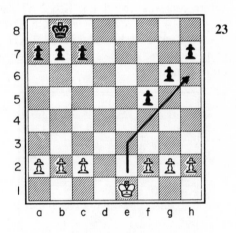

23

Schuster 1975

23. *The king is a powerful piece*. An instructive position. White wins because of a better-placed king and the weakness of Black's king-side pawns by making a beeline for h6; 1 Ke2 Kc8 2 Ke3 Kd7 3 Kf4 Ke6 (3 ... h6 4 Ke5! and eventually penetrates) 4 Kg5 Kf7 5 Kh6 Kg8 6 h4! followed by h5, breaking up the pawns. Black is forced to capture and then the f-pawn is up for grabs. One tempo makes all the difference here. If Black could answer Kf4 with Kf6 then it would be drawn.

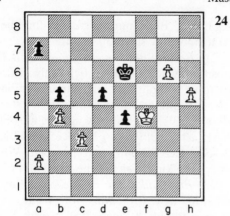

24

Bouaziz–Pomar, Siegen 1970

24. *Pawn power*. The well-advanced connected passed pawns give White tactical
opportunities, but Bouaziz played 1 g7?(=).
White can win with 1 h6! Kf6 2 h7 Kg7 3
Kg4! Kh8 4 Kf5 Kg7 (4 ... e3 5 Kf6 e2 6 Kf7
+−) 5 Ke6! e3 6 h8(Q)+ Kxh8 7 Kf7 and
mates in three. An idea which has been seen
more than once.

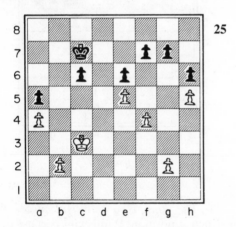

25

Omholt–Jensen – Smith, Oslo 1980

25. *Both sides now*. Black offered a draw
here, which was a little optimistic and a little
too late. White holds all the trumps in this
position and there are two winning plans at
her disposal. Creation of a D.P.P. with 1 b4
and sooner or later Black has to capture.
The alternative is a king-side breakthrough
with 1 g4 followed by an eventual f5, f6,
exf6, g5!.

LESSON 18. MINOR PIECE ENDINGS

The Case of the Bishop versus the Knight

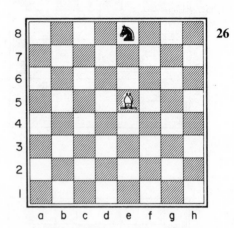

26

The Eternal Struggle

Nowadays it is generally agreed that the
bishop is the stronger piece. However,
Chigorin once asserted that the knight was
the more valuable and even today this
opinion gains some support. The bishop is a
mobile piece, capable of covering the board
in one move and simultaneously operating
on *both wings. It is able to lose* a move,
which the knight cannot (i.e. what the
knight does in an even number of moves it
cannot do in an odd number). The knight is
the drunken man of the chessboard, changing its focus and colour emphasis with each
leap. It rejoices in the firm foothold of an
outpost or *blockading station*. The bishop's
inherent disadvantage is that it controls
squares of only one colour and thus has no
effective power over half the board. The
knight may be its master in *blocked* pawn
situations or where the pawns are all on *one
wing* (i.e. where mobility is of less importance than manoeuvrability).

*In balanced situations, bishop vs. knight is
usually drawn* and *they are equally effective
at exploiting the advantage of a pawn plus.*

However, *where there is a positional advantage or passed pawns on both sides, the bishop is USUALLY better able to exploit this.*

In Practice

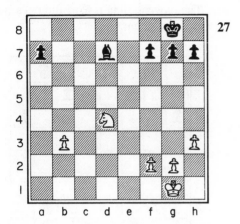

27

Black wins . . .

Stoltz–Kashdan, The Hague, 1921

This is a very beautiful and instructive ending which gives an elegant demonstration of the bishop's potential mastery in an *open* position with pawns on *both wings*. The first step is to *centralize the kings*.

1 ... Kf8 2 Kf1 Ke7 3 Ke2 Kd6 4 Kd3 Kd5 (Black scores the first point; his *king is better placed.* Now he intends to drive the king from d3 and *penetrate*) 5 h4 Bc8! 6 Nf3 Ba6+ 7 Kc3 (or 7 Ke3 Kc5 8 Ng5 Kb4 9 Nxf7 Kxb3 and the distant a-pawn will decide) 7 ... h6 8 Nd4 g6 9 Nc2 Ke4 10 Ne3 f5 11 Kd2 f4 12 Ng4 h5 13 Nf6+ Kf5 14 Nd7 (14 Nd5 Bb7 15 Ne7+ Kf6 16 Ng8+ Kf7 17 Nh6+ Kg7 −+) 14 ... Bc8! 15 Nf8 g5 16 g3 gxh4 17 gxh4 Kg4 18 Ng6 Bf5 19 Ne7 Be6 20 b4 Kxh4 21 Kd3 Kg4 22 Ke4 h4 23 Nc6 Bf5+ 24 Kd5 f3! (Now the h-pawn is unstoppable) 25 b5 h3 26 Nxa7 h2 27 b6 h1(Q) 28 Nc6 Qb1 29 Kc5 Be4 and White resigns.

Notice that after 6 ... Ba6+, White could not prevent Black's king from entering on either side.

The bishop is the only piece which is limited to squares of one colour, which explains why its strength is *so delicately related to the pawn-structure*. A "bad" bishop, which is hemmed in by its own pawns, can be a poor piece indeed. In the next diagram we see the knight as a hero, acting in its natural role as a *blockader* and dominating a "bad" bishop. Black has a P.P.P. which was of less than no use to him in the continuation:

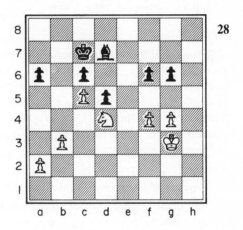

28

White wins . . .

Averbakh–Lilienthal, Moscow, 1949

1 g5! (to fix the black pawns on white squares) 1 ... fxg5 (1 ... f5 prevents the king's entry but leaves the bishop hopelessly bad and hands White a juicy *outpost* on e5, e.g. 2 Nf3 Be8 3 Ne5 Kd8 4 Kf3 Ke7 5 Ke3 Ke6 6 Kd4 Ke7 7 Nd3 Ke6 8 Nb4 a5 9 Nd3 Bd7 10 a4 Be8 11 b4 and the distant passed a-pawn will win). 2 fxg5 Bc8 3 Kf4 a5 4 Ke5 Ba6 5 Kf6 Bd3 6 Ke7! (6 Ne6+ and 7 Nf8 does not work as the Black d-pawn is then set free) 6 ... Bb1 7 a3 Be4 8 Ne6+ Kb7 9 Kd6 Bc2 10 Nd4 Bb1 11 Nxc6 +−.

Notice how White claimed total control over the black squares in the position. Also, the overall harmony between king, knight and pawns.

Despite all the theoretical talk of the respective qualities of bishops and knights, it is obvious that the decisive factor in both these positions was the winning side forcing a decisive *infiltration of the king*. THE KING is *by far the strongest piece in minor-piece endings*! The winning method is usually to create a passed-pawn — normally achieved by capturing one or two of the opponent's pawns!

Bishop vs. Bishop of Same Colour

Other things being equal, a material advantage will often suffice here. One pawn up will generally win (assuming enough pawns remain on the board) and even a positional edge may give strong possibilities. Because of the threat of *exchanging*, the weaker side is often faced with a gradual and painful retreat.

"That player has the advantage who can assail important points without his opponent daring to offer an exchange." — Lasker.

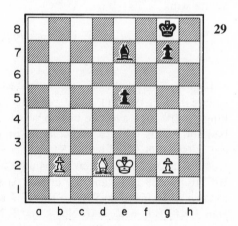

Lasker 1932

White plays and wins with the most minimal of means. 1 Bc3 Bd6 2 Ke3 Kf7 3 Ke4 Ke6 4 b4 Bc7 5 b5 and Black runs out of moves: 5 ... Kf6 6 g4 Ke6 7 g5 g6 8 Bb2 Bd6 9 b6 Bb8 (or 9 ... Bc5 10 b7 Bd6 11 Ba3 Bb8

12 Bc5 Kd7 13 Kd5 e4 14 Be3! with an imminent exchange of bishops) 10 Ba3 Kd7 11 Bf8! Ke6 12 Bg7 Bd6 13 Bf6! Bb8 14 Bd8 and White forces the exchange of bishops.

White has the D.P.P. and weak point (e5) to attack; it is amazing that this is enough to win. The pawn ending is won and because of this so is the game.

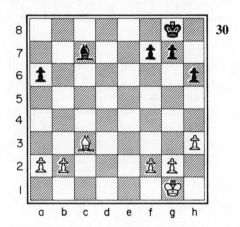

Fine 1941

Notice how easily White wins here. The play follows three logical stages; (1) centralization, (2) creation of passed pawn, (3) sacrifice of pawn as decoy to win on kingside — exactly the same strategy as would apply in the corresponding pawn ending.

1 ... g6 2 Kf1 Kf8 3 Ke2 Ke7 4 Kd3 Kd6 5 Kc4 Kc6 6 b4 Bb6 7 f3 Bc7 8 a4 Bb6 9 Bd4! Bc7 10 b5+ axb5+ 11 axb5+ Kb7 12 Kd5 Bb8 13 Bf2! Bc7 14 g3 h5 15 h4 Bb8 16 b6 and Black has run out of moves (1–0).

Minor piece endings occur very regularly in practice and bishop vs. bishop of same colour is one of the *easiest to handle*. One should be wary of entering such situations with a definite positional or material disadvantage as the counter-chances are slight. The basic ingredients are the same as with pawn-endings; P.P.P., D.P.P., king position and pawn weaknesses are of great significance with the added theme of "good" vs. "bad" bishop.

Bishop vs. Bishop of Opposite Colour

This is a notoriously *drawish ending, even when one side has a material plus.* The fact that the bishops can never be opposed means that the possibility of exchanging down to a clearer pawn ending is slight and the defending side can often set up an unbreachable *blockade*. In an otherwise normal situation, one pawn up will generally *not* win unless it is accompanied by a positional advantage. In odd cases sometimes two or even three pawns will not do the trick. The most important factors here are *passed pawns* and the possibility of creating them. The two most common winning methods are creating a pair of *mobile* connected passed pawns, or two *widely separated* passed pawns which will force the defender to sacrifice the bishop.

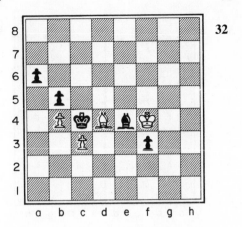

Calder–Smith – Katz, London, 1949

Knight vs. Knight Endings

Here again, *one pawn extra will normally suffice to win.* The knight, however, is a crazy beast and its penchant for unpredictable tactics means that this is often a difficult ending to conduct.

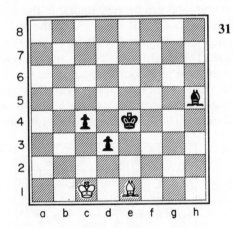

Drawn. The black bishop has no power over the vital squares c3 and d2. [*N.B.* If Black's king were on d4 and the pawn advanced to c3 then it is easily won as long as ... c2??, allowing another blockade, is avoided!].

In the next diagram Black to play wins outright by threatening to create another passed pawn with 1 ... a5!! 0–1.

If 2 Kxe4 a4 3 Be3 a3 4 Bc1 f2. Or 2 bxa5 b4 3 Kxe4 b3 4 a6 b2, queening with check.

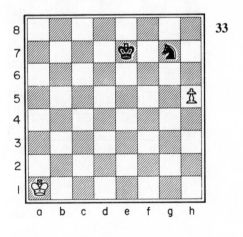

Helpless

The diagram demonstrates a peculiar difficulty in stopping a passed pawn, especially the rook pawn. 1 h6 Kf7 2 h7! +–.

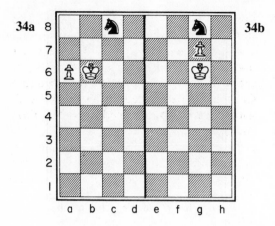

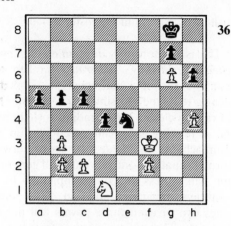

Bonner–Medina, Haifa, 1980

The forker. Here the knight impresses by single-handedly stopping a passed pawn. Its ability to *fork* saves the situation in Diagram 34a. 1 Kc7 Na7 2 Kb7 Nb5 3 Kb6 Nd6! 4 a7 Nc8+ (=).

Similarly Black is safe in Diagram 34b, as the knight holds the queening square.

Tactics come to the fore. Black to play made a sealed move, choosing the brilliant and decisive 1 ... Nc3!!, when the a-pawn romps home.

(2 bxc3 a4 3 cxd4 cxd4! 4 Nb2 a3 −+).

Knight endings are often likened to pawn endings and can be very similar in the sense that the positional weapons of the *P.P.P. and especially the D.P.P. are very potent here*. The knight may act effectively enough in the role of blockader against the former, but such a short-stepping beast has great problems keeping an eye on a wing-pawn. Here is a classical example of this theme.

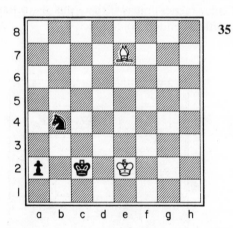

Stein–Dorfmann, USSR, 1973

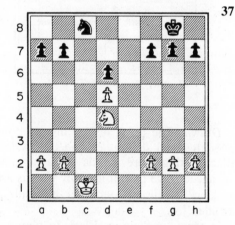

Alekhine–Andersen, Folkestone, 1933

Here the knight depresses by its inability to lose a move. 1 Bf6 Nd3 2 Ba1 Nb2 3 Ke1 Kb1 4 Kd2 Kxa1 5 Kc1 Nc4 6 Kc2 and the knight is powerless to help extricate the king (=). (White must only remember to go to a square of the same colour as the knight. 5 Kc2? loses).

Alekhine's winning plan is to convert his spatial advantage and better knight into the advantage of a D.P.P. by swapping his d-pawn for one of Black's queen-side pawns.

1 Nb3! Kf8 (1 ... Ne7 2 Na5 Nxd5 3 Nxb7 Nb4 4 Nxd6 Nd3+ (4 ... Nxa2+ 5 Kc2 Nb4+ 6 Kc3 and the white king enters quickly) 5 Kc2 Nxf2 6 b4! Kf8 7 b5 +−) 2 Na5 b6 3 Nc6 Ke8 4 Kd2 Ne7 5 Nxa7 Nxd5 6 Nb5 Kd7 7 Nd4 g6 8 a4 Nc7 9 Kc3 g5 10 Kb4 d5 11 Nf3 f6 12 Nd4 Kd6? (Loses quickly, but on 12 ... Ke7 13 a5 bxa5+ 14 Kxa5 Kd7 15 b4 Kc8 16 Kb6 +−) 13 Nb5+ Nxb5 14 Kxb5 Ke5 15 b4 d4 16 Kc4 (1–0).

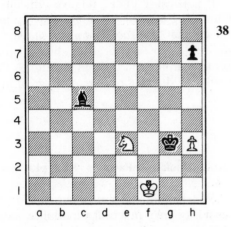

Rellstab–Machate, Essen, 1948

The "wrong" bishop. 1 Kg1! Bxe3+ 2 Kh1(=). To win with bishop plus rook pawn vs. king the bishop must be of the *same colour* as the pawn's queening square (with odd exceptions). This explains the combination. White can now happily sit tight in the corner, sure in the knowledge that Black has no more than stalemate.

LESSON 19. ROOK AND PAWN ENDINGS

These are by far the most common endings to occur in practical play, and any serious student could reap benefit from a study of some of the difficulties involved. The rook becomes a mighty force in the ending, capable of producing tactical and positional ideas of great richness. Perhaps this is why it was Bobby Fischer's declared favourite piece — an interesting choice. The distinguishing mark of being able to control a *whole rank or file* puts it on a level far above the minor pieces in both *power of action and confusion of effect*. It is said that Capablanca (renowned for his precise end-game technique) examined over 1000 rook and pawn endings before developing his great flair for them. All this may sound a little daunting, but here we shall limit ourselves to only 18 positions which should amply repay a little time and patience.

Basic Situations

One fundamental point is that king plus rook is a sufficient *mating force*. This gives importance to the struggle of rook vs. pawns. King plus rook vs. king plus pawn will win easily unless the pawn is far advanced. King plus rook vs. king plus two pawns generally wins — though it is worth remembering that *two connected passed pawns on the sixth rank are normally worth at least a rook*.

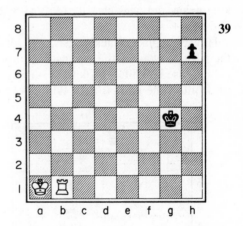

Fine 1941

White's king is very badly placed, but there is still a win with 1 Rg1+! (gaining a *tempo*) 1 ... Kf5 (the only square, note 1 ... Kh5? 2 Kb2 is easy) 2 Rh1 Kg6 3 Kb2 h5 4 Kc3 Kg5 5 Kd2 Kg4 6 Ke2 h4 7 Kf2 h3 8 Rh2 Kh4 9 Kf3 +−. Black to move draws with 1 ... h5. A classic maxim is that *rooks belong behind passed pawns, whether your own or your opponent's!* If White could play 1 Rh8 in the diagram then he would win easily enough.

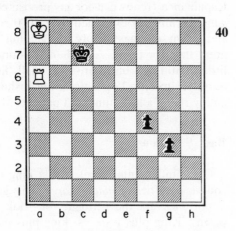

Sozin 1935

Black's king is *cut off* from the dangerous passed pawns and with accurate play White wins. 1 Rg6! (holding both pawns) 1 ... Kd7 2 Rg4! g2 3 Rxg2 Ke6 4 Rg5! cuts off the king again and wins clearly. (4 ... f3 5 Rg3 f2 6 Rf3 +−).

However, place Black's f-pawn on f3 and then Black *wins* as the pawns are unstoppable. Also if White's rook were on, say, a1 (in front of the pawns) then White is lost.

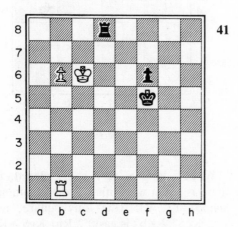

Alekhine–Bogolyubov,
World Championship, 1929

An example of how these positions may arise. Bogolyubov failed to find the saving clause:
1 ... Kg4? 2 b7 f5 3 b8(Q) Rxb8 4 Rxb8 f4 5 Kd5 f3 6 Ke4 f2 7 Rf8 +−.

Black, however, could have drawn by using the king to push the pawn and *also* prevent the approach of White's king, i.e. 1 ... Ke4! 2 b7 f5 3 b8(Q) Rxb8 4 Rxb8 f4 5 Re8+ Kd4! 6 Rf8 Ke3 7 Kd5 f3 (=).

It is because of the relative difficulty of converting a small advantage that we hear the cry that *"All rook and pawn endings are drawn!"*. This is not true, but is worth bearing in mind in difficult situations. Certainly the drawing resources are great in:

King, Rook and Pawn vs. King plus Rook

We shall look at this in reasonable detail as it is of great practical importance and can also be a big help in understanding more complicated positions. The basic ending is normally *drawn if* the defending king can *block the pawn or occupy its queening square*. In all cases, White (the attacking side) tries to *cut off* the opposing king. A helpful formula discovered by Philidor is that the defending side should place the rook on the *third rank* to prevent the advance of White's king. When the pawn goes to the *sixth*, Black's rook goes to the *eighth* in order to threaten repeated checks at a safe distance. The rook pawn is, as ever, drawish. Against a knight pawn Black should *not* allow the king to be driven away. Against a c-, d-, e- or f-pawn Black can move to the *shorter* side and still draw. As with all rules, there are exceptions. Nevertheless, these are useful and practical guides.

Some examples:

King, rook and knight pawn vs. *king plus rook*. The position in Diagram 42 is drawn.
1 ... Rg6! (1 ... Rg8 would also draw

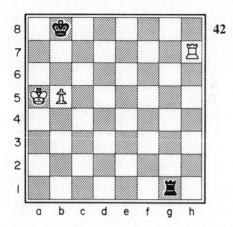

42

King, rook and bishop pawn vs. *king plus rook.*

When Philidor's method is out, Black still draws against a bishop's (or centre) pawn by *putting the rook on the eighth*. Passive defence does *not* work here as White's rook can operate on both sides of the pawn.

1 ... Rg1! 2 Kb6 Rc1! 3 Kc6 Kb8 (Black moves to the *shorter* side, the point being that the rook now has more room to check from the longer side) 4 Rh8+ Ka7 5 Rc8 (On 5 Rd8 Rc2 waiting, or 5 Kd6 Kb7) 5 ... Rh1 6 Kd7 Rh7+ 7 Kc6 Rh6+ 8 Kb5 Kb7 9 Rg8 Kc7 10 Rg7+ Kc8 with Philidor's position (=). Alternatively White could try 2 Kc6 Kb8! 3 Rh8+ Ka7 4 Rd8 Rc1! (When checks are not practicable, Black attacks the pawn from behind) 5 Kd6 Kb7 (the king moves back) 6 Rd7+ Kc8 7 Rc7+ Kb8 8 Rh7 Rc2 9 c6 Rd2+ (=).

White to play *wins* as Black is forced to remain *passive*. Let us see what happens then. 1 Kb6 Kb8 (1 ... Rg1 2 Rh8+ Kd7 3 c6+ Kd6 4 Rd8+ Ke7 5 c7 +−) 2 c6 Rf8 3 Rh7 Re8 4 Rb7+ Kc8 5 Ra7 Kb8 6 c7+ Kc8 7 Ra8+ +−.

here, but not against a bishop's or centre pawn) 2 Rf7 Rh6 3 b6 Rh1! 4 Ka6 Ra1+. Now we see what happens when the pawn has *reached the sixth. White can only avoid checks at the cost of his pawn.*

White to play can create threats with 1 Ka6 Rg8!! (against a knight pawn Black *loses* if by keeping the rook on the 8th rank he allows the king to be driven away. Instructive blunders are: 1 ... Rb1? 2 Kb6 Kc8 — with the knight pawn there is no *shorter* side to go to — 3 Rh8+ Kd7 4 Rb8! Rb2 5 Ka7 Kc7 6 b6+ Kc6 7 Rc8+ Kd7 8 b7 Ra2+ 9 Kb8 reaching the *Lucena position* which is examined later. Also, if 1 ... Kc8? 2 Rh8+ Kd7 3 b6 etc.) 2 b6 Rf8 and White can do nothing against Black's totally passive defence.

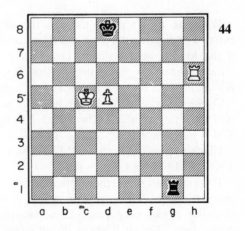

44

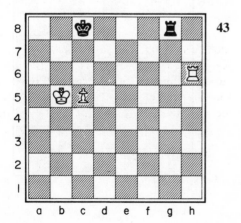

43

With a *centre pawn*: 1 Kd6 Kc8! 2 Rh8+ Kb7 3 Ke7 Rg7+ 4 Kd8 (4 Ke8 Kc7 5 Rh6 Rg8+ 6 Ke7 Rg7+ 7 Ke6 Rd7 8 Rh5 Rd6+ (=)) 4 ... Rg6! 5 Rh5 (5 Rh7+ Kb6 6 Rd7 Kc5 7 Kc7 Rh6 8 Rd8 Rh7+ 9 Kb8 Rh6) 5 ... Rd6+ 6 Ke7 Kc7 7 Re5 Rd7+ 8 Ke6 Rd6+ 9 Kf7 Rd7+ 10 Re7 Kd6 (=).

From the defending side's point of view the following must be avoided: (1) the rook being passive (except in the case of the knight's pawn) (2) the king being driven away unnecessarily (3) moving to the wrong side when/if driven away. The defender must also know when it is correct to attack the pawn from behind and when to use the rook to check from the flanks.

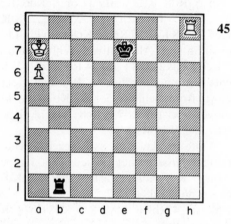

With the rook's pawn there is the difficulty of extricating the king and Black draws if the king is near enough. Diagram 45 is critical. White to play wins: 1 Rb8! Rc1 2 Kb7 Kd6 (2 ... Rb1+ 3 Ka8 Ra1 4 a7 Kd6 5 Kb7 +−) 3 a7 Rb1+ 4 Kc8 Rc1+ 5 Kd8 Rh1 (With a threat!) 6 Rb6+ Kc5 7 Rc6+! Kb4 8 Rc8 Rh8+ 9 Kc7 Rh7+ 10 Kb8 +−.

Black to play draws: 1 ... Kd7 2 Rb8 Ra1 3 Kb7 Rb1+ 4 Ka8 Ra1 5 Kb7 (=).

If you find all this rather difficult then you are not alone! These positions are worth studying for that very reason as such endings occur daily and yet there is no all-purpose formula to cover all cases.

We have seen how Black draws typical situations, but if White successfully manages to escort his pawn to the 7th rank then there is still one more bridge to be crossed, which leads us to:

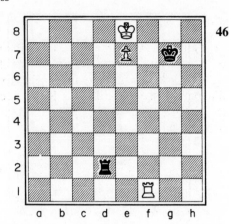

The Lucena Position

. . . Or how to build a bridge. The problem is how to create a shelter for the white king to escape from checks. 1 Rg1+ Kh7 2 Rg4! (Rg5 also wins) 2 ... Rf2 3 Kd7 Rd2+ 4 Ke6 Re2+ 5 Kd6 Rd2+ 6 Ke5 Re2+ 7 Re4 +−.

This is a *fundamental* idea which occurs often. There is also a more mundane winning line, *viz.* 1 Rg1+ Kh7 2 Ra1 Kg7 3 Ra8 Rd1 4 Rd8 Re1 5 Kd7 Rd1+ 6 Kc6 and Black runs out of checks.

Ideas and Positional Themes

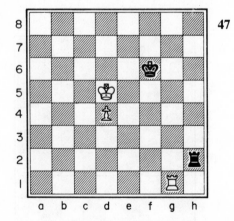

Cut off the King

It should not be hard to see the winning move for White now. 1 Re1! cuts off the king and White can mentally chalk up a point on the scoreboard (1 ... Rh8 2 Kc6! Rc8+ 3 Kd7 +−).

Black to move draws with 1 ... Ke7.

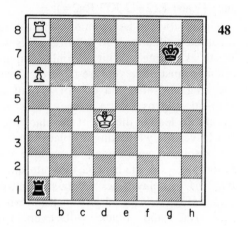

48

A Place to Hide

49. White must not play a hasty 1 a7?? in the diagram as that square is needed to shelter from checks. How many won games have been drawn through a premature pawn push to the 7th in similar situations! 1 Kc5 Kf7 2 Kb6 Rb1+ 3 Ka7 Ke7 4 Rb8 Ra1 5 Kb7 Rb1+ 6 Ka8 Ra1 7 a7 Kd7 8 Kb7 Rb1+ 9 Ka6 Ra1+ 10 Kb6 Rb1+ 11 Kc5 +−.

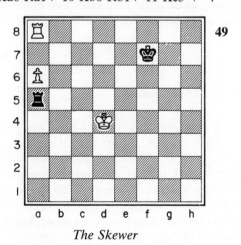

49

The Skewer

1 a7?(=) Ke7? 2 Rh8! +− (2 ... Rxa7 3 Rh7+). The point to notice after 1 a7 is that Black's king must remain on either g7 or h7 (avoiding Rh8 or else a rook check followed by a8(Q)).

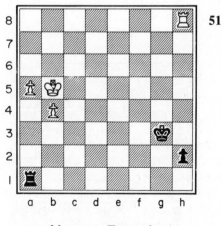

50

Kmoch 1959

Seventh Heaven

50. White obviously holds an advantage here as the rook has found its natural home on the *7th rank*. What is less obvious is that, given time, Black may well equalize through 1 ... g6, 2 ... Kf8, 3 ... Ke8, expelling the unwelcome visitor.

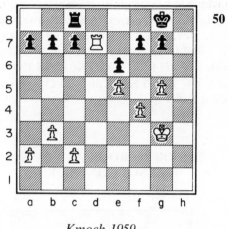

51

Maroczy–Tarrasch

Lust to Expand

1 g6! (to make inroads with the king and also open up the 7th rank) 1 ... fxg6 2 Kg4 b5? (makes things easy, though Black cannot avoid creating weaknesses indefinitely) 3 Kg5 Kh7 4 Re7 Rd8 5 Rxe6 Rd2 6 Rc6 +−. Tactical exploitation of a positional advantage is a common theme.

51. Maroczy played 1 Kc6 Rc1+ 2 Kb6 Rc4! (threat 3 ... Rh4) 3 Rxh2 Rxb4+ 4 Kc5 Ra4 (=), missing a straightforward win with 1 Rxh2! Kxh2 2 Ka6 Kg3 3 b5 Kf4 4 b6 Ke5 5 b7 Rb1 6 Ka7 Kd6 7 b8(Q)+ Rxb8 8 Kxb8 Kc6 9 a6 +−.

LESSON 20. ROOK AND PAWN ENDINGS CONTINUED

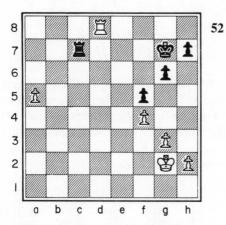

Rooks belong behind passed pawns

Correct strategy for White in Diagram 52 is 1 Rd2!! followed by Ra2 +− when Black's rook will be reduced to total passivity. This type of position occurs very often in practical play and the respective rooks' positions is often of *decisive* importance (1 a6? Rc2+ 2 Kf3 Ra2=).

The position in Diagram 53 demonstrates a common situation and the strategy is well worth knowing. White's only winning attempt must be to venture towards a7 with the king and abandon one or two of the king-side pawns to the wolves. This may eventually lead to the win of the black rook, but leaves the white king misplaced to fight the resultant counterplay. A sample continuation . . . 1 Kf3 h5 2 Ke4 (White should try 2 h4 to delay Black's king-side pawns) 2 ... Rxf2 3 Rc8 Ra2 4 Rc6 (4 Ra8 Rxh2 5 Kd5 Ra2 and Black will even win) 4 ... Rxh2 5 Kd5 Ra2 6 Kc5 g5 7 Kb6 h4 8 gxh4 gxh4 9 a7 h3 10 Kb7 h2 11 Rc1 Rb2+ 12 Kc6 Ra2 13 Kb7 (=). If the positions of the rooks in the diagram are reversed, then of course *White wins*. White has chances in positions like this when the black pawns are too advanced (e.g. f5, g4, h5) leaving the king exposed, or are weak and subject to capture. Common sense tells us that White has much greater possibilities with a b-pawn, as then the king saves two moves on its return queen-side excursion.

Game Continuations

A great watchword of all rook and pawn endings is that of *activity*. The rook is essentially an *attacking* piece and to perform the menial task of passively defending is usually beneath its dignity. To be forced into such a situation does not necessarily mean the eventual loss of the game, but it is often a *big step in the wrong direction*!

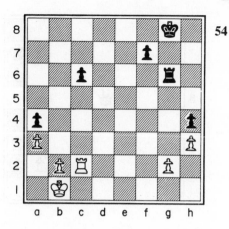

Van de Hoek–Euwe

Passed pawns must be pushed. "One has never lost as long as one can offer some threat." — Euwe. This is a good example of active counterplay and the potential *power of the passed pawn.* Black falls two pawns behind here but still draws. 1 Rc4 Rxg2 2 Rxa4 f5 (Black's only counterplay is the passed f-pawn on which all energies are concentrated) 3 Rxh4 Kf7 4 Rh6 f4! 5 Rxc6 f3 6 Rc4 f2 7 Rf4+ Ke6 8 Ka2 Ke5 9 Rf8 Ke4 10 a4 Ke3 (Threatening ... Rg3 ... Rf3) 11 Re8+ Kd3 12 Rd8+ Ke3 13 Re8+ and *drawn* by repetition.

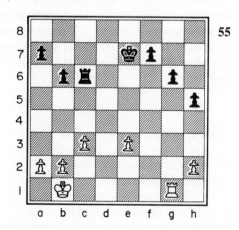

Schlechter–Rubinstein, San Sebastian, 1912

Black to Play and Win

Rubinstein was regarded as the incomparable master of rook endings. Here is one of his famous masterpieces which gives a good illustration of active vs. passive rook.
1 ... Re6 2 Re1 Rf6 3 Re2 Ke6 4 Kc2 Ke5 5 c4 Ke4 6 b4 g5 7 Kc3 g4 8 c5 h4 9 Rg2 Rg6 10 Kc4 g3 11 hxg3 hxg3 12 Kb5 bxc5 13 bxc5 Kf3 14 Rg1 a6+! (0–1). After 15 Kc4 g2 16 Kd5 Kf2 it is easy.

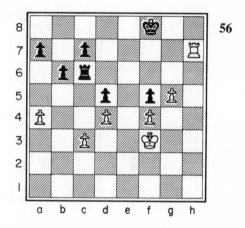

Capablanca–Tartakower, New York, 1924

Seventh Absolute

Capablanca, also, made his niche in this department. Here he gives a textbook lesson on the power of the 7th rank, active king and passed pawn(s). 1 Kg3! Rxc3+ 2 Kh4 Rf3 (Fine suggests 2 ... Rc1! as tougher) 3 g6 Rxf4+ 4 Kg5 Re4 5 Kf6! (sidestepping the black pawn) Kg8 6 Rg7+ Kh8 7 Rxc7 Re8 8 Kxf5 Re4 9 Kf6 Rf4+ 10 Ke5 Rg4 11 g7+ Kg8 12 Rxa7 Rg1 13 Kxd5 and White soon won.

Queen and Pawn Endings

The queen's immense power and capacity to set up double-attack, perpetual check or mating situations means that these endings are potentially the most difficult. The fact that (in a straight queen vs. queen fight) *a lone queen can escort a pawn home to its promotion square* explains why *passed pawns* and the possibility of creating them can be *very important* here. One well-advanced passed pawn may outweigh a large material disadvantage. A pawn advantage may often be enough to win but its exploitation will still require great patience and tactical vigilance.

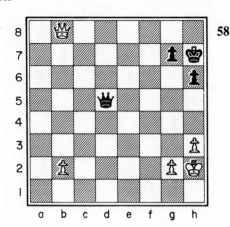

from queening. Black can only throw his king-side pawns forward with the idea of gaining perpetual check; however, this is a vain hope.

Space limitations do not allow us to enter into a discussion of the very technical endings of bishop and knight mate, king and queen vs. king and rook, etc., which the keen student may cull from any larger text on the endings.

> "Imagination is of little use in the ending. This is the domain of the artisan rather than the artist."

We leave the reader to dwell on the accuracy of this quote. Hopefully, this brief introduction will have helped in the assimilation of some of the purely technical ideas which must be digested before imagination can freely play its part — for surely imagination must always play a part — even in the ending.

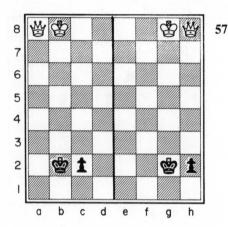

The queen will always win against king plus pawn on the 7th except in the well-known cases of king plus rook pawn or king plus bishop pawn. In both these cases the defending side has the resource of *stalemate*. The student should play out these and examples with other pawns. [*N.B.* White may still win if the king is close enough to create a mating net (see Diagram 20).]

The theoretical stance on king, queen plus pawn versus king plus queen has changed in recent years. Many positions that were once dismissed as draws have now been proved to be wins and the task of defending such positions is often very arduous. A detailed study of queen plus pawn endings is beyond the scope of this work, but Diagram 58 is an example of one recurrent theme which is of great practical importance.

White plays 1 b4 and wins rather easily as Black has no means of preventing this pawn

Bibliography

Recommended, General and Reference Works

R. Fine, *Basic Chess Endings*, McKay.
Euwe and Hooper, *A Guide to Chess Endings*, Routledge and Kegan Paul.
Keres, *Practical Chess Endings*, Batsford.
Averbakh, *Chess Endings: Essential Knowledge*, Pergamon Press.

Others

Hooper, *Practical Chess End-Games*, Routledge and Kegan Paul.
Chernev, *Practical Chess Endings*, Faber & Faber.
Schuster, *End-games in Chess*, Lutterworth Press.
Barden, *How to Play the End-game in Chess*, Bobbs & Merrill.

Advanced and Supplementary

Nunn, *Tactical Chess Endings*, Allen & Unwin.
Speelman, *Analysing the End-game*, Batsford.

EXERCISES I: Lessons 5–8. How to Analyse a Position

In each of the following seven diagrammed positions there is either a correct plan which leads to victory or a precise forcing sequence which is decisive. Use the themes highlighted in the lessons to help you find the solutions. All positions except no. 3 are White to move.

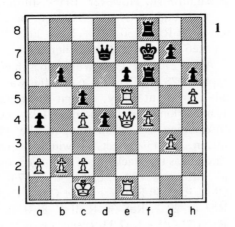

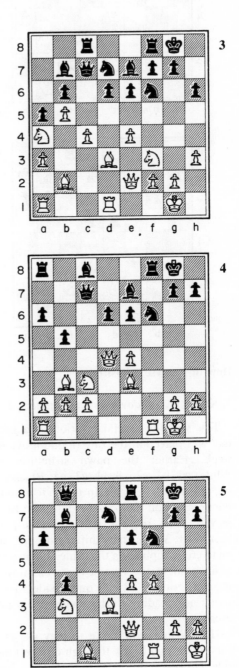

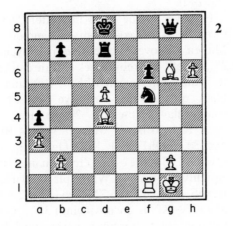

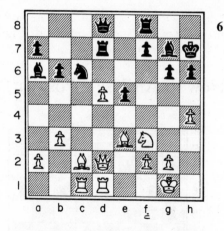

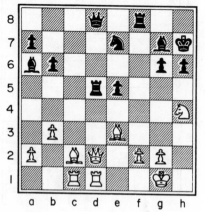

How to Analyse a Position

1. *Kopec vs. Sunday Standard Readers, 1982*

This was the crucial position of a game that was played at the rate of one move per week. Earlier the pawn structure was White: a2, b2, c2, c3, f4, g3, h4; Black: a4, b6, c5, d7, e6, g7, h7. In order to remove the pressure on the backward d-pawn Black played ... d5 thereby leaving the e-pawn backward. White then shifted the pressure on to e6 by tripling on the e-file. Then at the right moment the lever c4! struck, forcing the disruption of Black's queen-side 5-pawn group and leading to the diagrammed position.

Here White would like to play g4–g5 to burst open and break through on the king-side. However, if now 27 g4 then 27 ... Kg8!

would provide Black with sufficient counter-play against the f-pawn to gain equality, e.g. 28 Rxe6 Rxe6 29 Qxe6+ Qxe6 30 Rxe6 Rxf4 31 Rxb6 Rxg4 with Black certainly not worse in the rook plus pawn ending; or if 28 Rf1 to keep the status quo with pressure, then 28 ... Qf7 forces matters. So White needs to prevent ... Kg8 if he is to play g4 with the threat of g5 to immediately follow.

The only move which achieves this objective is 27 Qh7! but it does involve some risks in that the white queen is thereby highly decentralized. Black could reply with 27 ... Qc6 threatening ... Qf3. Now on 28 g4 Rxf4 29 g5 would lead to a decisive breakthrough. However, Black still has 28 ... Qf3! and on 29 g5? Qxf4+ or on 29 f5 Qxg4 30 Rxe6 (30 fxe6+ Ke7) 30 ... Rxe6 31 fxe6+ Ke7 and Black is better.

After 27 Qh7 Qc6 White does have a reply in 28 R1e4! which paves the way for g4–g5 without delay, though the road to Rome is long and treacherous. If 28 ... Qc8 threatening 29 ... Rh8 trapping the white queen, 29 f5! effects a winning break-through as the black queen no longer covers g6. If now 29 ... exf5 30 Re7+ or 29 ... Rxf5 30 Rxf5+ exf5 31 Qg6+ Kg8 32 Re7 or 29 ... Re8 30 Rg4! Rg8 31 fxe6+ Rxe6 32 Qf5+ Ke7 33 Rxe6+ Qxe6 34 Re4 or finally if in the last line 32 ... Rf6 33 Rxg7+!!.

However in the main line after 27 Qh7 Qc6 28 R1e4 co-authors Chandler and Mullen discovered the fine improvement 28 ... Qa8! whereby Black still threatens to trap the white queen with ... Rh8 and the black queen keeps an "eye" on h1 for counterplay. Now on 29 f5 Re8 (on 29 ... Rh8 30 fxe6+ wins) if 30 Rg4 Black has 30 ... Qh1+ 31 Kd2 Qg2+ 32 Re2 Qxe2+!! 33 Kxe2 exf5+ etc. with more than equality. If instead White plays 30 fxe6+ Rexe6 31 Rxe6 Rxe6 32 Rxe6 (32 Qf5+ Rf6 33 Qd7+ Kf8 is unconvincing) 32 ... Qh1+ (an important intermezzo which stems from 28 ... Qa8!) 33 Kd2 Kxe6 and Black draws the queen-ending without difficulty. White could instead bide his time with 30 g4 when Black can do nothing positive, but with the white queen amusingly stalemated and g5 not a threat, neither can White do anything positive.

Thus a further assessment of the initial diagrammed position leads one to conclude that if White plays 27 a3!! Black is virtually in zugzwang! His pawns cannot move, except for 1 ... g6 which is very weakening. His rooks cannot move, as for example the rook on f8 must remain put to meet 28 g4 with ... Kg8. The black king and black queen must guard e6 and 28 ... Qc8 is again decisively met by f5! Only 27 ... Qd6 requires further consideration. The move 27 a3!! not only passes the onus of moving to Black, but also creates an important flight square for the white king. Hence after 27 ... Qd6 28 Kb1! leaves Black at a loss for a move since the variations given earlier with a check on h1 by the black queen are no longer significant. If here 28 ... Rb8 White wins with simply 29 g4 and 30 g5. If 28 ... Qd7 White proceeds with the earlier idea of 29 Qh7, e.g. 29 ... Qc6 30 Rle4 Qa8 31 f5 Re8 32 Rg4 winning easily.

Admittedly all these ramifications of 27 Qh7 would have been difficult to analyse in over-the-board play. The game concluded 27 Qh7 Rb8? 28 g4 Rxf4 29 g5 hxg5 30 h6 Rg8 31 Rxe6 resigns.

Summary. Having found that the threat of g4–g5 was decisive, and realizing that Black had no threats, it was necessary to find a sound way to effect this threat. 27 Qh7 was the right idea but premature due to the saving clause 28 ... Qa8!. However, after the calm 27 a3!! it quickly becomes apparent that Black is in virtual zugzwang and then after 28 Kb1! White can ruthlessly carry out his threat.

2. *Kopec–C. McNab, Edinburgh Congress 1981*

This position with White momentarily a queen down for bishop and two pawns, was reached after Black's 38th move (Rd6xd7).

White could simply play 39 Bxf5 and remain with two bishops and two pawns for a queen as he has for the past 20 moves or so. A continuation could then go: 39 ... Qxd5 40 Bxf6+ Kc7 41 Rc1+ (not 41 h7? Qc5+ 42 Kh1 Rxh7+ 43 Bxh7 Qh5+ etc.) and even though he retains winning chances it's not all that clear.

However, through a precise series of *intermezzo* checks and deadly strokes, Black's next four moves can be forced causing havoc amongst his pieces: 39 Bb6+!! (never miss a good check, but not 39 Bxf6+ Kc7 (39 ... Ne7 loses to 40 h7 and 39 ... Re7 to 40 Bxf5) 40 Bxf5 Qxd5 transposing to the note above) 39 ... Ke7 (if 39 ... Kc8 40 Bxf5 is crushing) 40 h7! (taking advantage of this precise moment when the black king interferes with the black rook's defence of h7 to let the pawn gain in strength) 40 ... Qg7 (after 40 ... Qxg6 41 h8=Q with a new queen and the black king still wide open White would win easily) 41 Re1+! Kd6 (now the black king interferes with the black rook's attack on the d-pawn) 42 Bxf5 (only now does White capture the knight, harassing Black's rook threatening Re8, and so forcing his reply) 42 ... Re7 43 Rxe7! (not 43 Bc5+?? Kxc5 44 Rxe7 Qxe7 45 h8=Q for Black has 45 ... Qe1+ followed by 46 ... Qe5+ picking up the bishop) 43 ... Kxe7 44 Bc5+ Kf7 (the black king is now a little bit schizoid, since he wants to help stop both of White's passed pawns but is caught between them and can stop neither. On 44 ... Kd8 or 44 ... Ke8 after 45 d6 the pawn will advance with check) 45 d6 Qh6 46 d7 Qc1+ 47 Kh2 Qf4+ 48 Kh1 Qh4+ 49 Bh3 f5 50 h8=Q Qxh8 51 Bb6 Qxb2 52 d8=Q. White promotes for the second time and this time the queen is to stay. Black should resign, but played on for seven more moves.

Moral. Never miss a check, especially if it's part of a forcing sequence. If you see a good move, look for a better one leading to positions which you feel are simpler and easier for you to play or win.

3. *Najdorf–Reshevsky, Match 1952*

(Black to move: also appears as example no. 22 of the Bratko–Kopec Experiment in *Advances in Computer Chess* **3**, 1982, Pergamon Press).

The winning continuation from the diagrammed position is actually quite simple, short, and straightforward — once you've seen it. However, it is unusual enough that only one of 35 humans graded between 1600 and 2400 found it (I.M. Craig Pritchett). People suggest all kinds of reasonable and interesting continuations such as ... d5!?, ... Rfd8, ... Rfe8, ... Nh5, ... Ne5!?, and ... e5!?. Such moves fall into the typical strategical lines of play in "hedgehog positions", but the solution is: 1 ... Bxe4! 2 Bxe4 Qxc4 3 Qxc4 Rxc4 and wins back the piece remaining at least a clear pawn ahead. The combination is based on the overloaded white queen and hanging knight on a4. Note that the move order inversion 1 ... Nxe4? does not work. A pity that after playing the winning combination Reshevsky later blundered and only drew.

How many of you kicked yourselves after seeing how simple it is? Never mind, you are in good company, as a former World Champion (in 1952) suggested the provocative ... e5!?.

4. *Rogolowicz–Jarecz*

(Also appears as example number 5 of the Bratko–Kopec Experiment)

This position tests a player's experience as much as anything else for the stock Sicilian sacrifice, 1 Nd5! is called for here. The analysis could go: 1 Nd5 Nxd5 (if 1 ... exd5 2 Bxd5+ etc.) 2 Rxf8+ (an important intermezzo improving on Informant 18's solution, Ex. No. 24, where after 2 Bxd5 Rb8 3 Qa7 Bd8! (a move found by M. Condie) is not decisive) 2 ... Kxf8 (if 2 ... Bxf8 now 3 Bxd5 Rb8 4 Qa7 +−); now there are two continuations of interest to White:

(a) 3 exd5! e5 4 Qe4 Kg8 (on 4 ... h6 5 Bxh6! followed by Qg6 wins; or 4 ... g6!? 5 Rf1+ Kg7 6 Qf3 Bb7 7 Qf7+ Kh8 8 Bh6 Rg8 9 Kh1! with great pressure as Black can hardly move while White improves his position through c3, Bc2–e4. 5 Qxe5!! dxe5 6 d6+ Qc4 7 Bxc4+ bxc4 8 dxe7 and White should win.

(b) The more brutal line is 3 Bxd5!? exd5 (3 ... Rb8 4 Bh6 exd5 5 Qxg7+ Ke8 6 exd5 with a strong attack) 4 Rf1+ Bf6 (if 4 ... Ke8 5 Qxg7 with decisive threats) 5 e5! dxe5 6 Qxd5 +− as Black has no defence to 7 Bc5+ with deadly threats, e.g. 6 ... Ra7 7 Kh1 etc.

For those who like quieter methods, sixteen-year-old Mark Condie contributed the strong lever, 1 a4! as another way to proceed.

Summary. It requires a certain amount of chess culture (experience) to play the typical "Sicilian sacrifice" 1 Nd5! without necessarily being able to see all its ramifications; 1 a4 is a good positional alternative.

5. *Pritchett–Gheorghiu, Lloyd's Bank Masters, London, 1980*

White has sacrificed a pawn for the two bishops and king-side attacking chances. There is no time to be wasted as Black might be able to organize a defence by playing ... e5 and his connected queen-side passed pawns may soon become dangerous. Pritchett continued: 23 e5 Nd5 24 Qh5 Nf8 (Black's last two moves were virtually forced) 25 f5! (White uses his trump, a king-side majority, to add more fuel to the fire) 25 ... exf5 26 Qxf5 Qc7 27 Nc5! (taking advantage of the black queen's load in defending f7 and creating numerous threats including 28 Bc4) 27 ... Bc8 28 Qf3 (the white knight and e-pawn are still immune while White steps up the pressure by attacking the hanging black knight on d5) 28 ... Nb6 29 e6! (new threats as the pawn advances with immunity, e.g. 29 ... Bxe6 30 Qxf8+! Rxf8 31 Rxf8+ Kxf8 32 Nxe6+ wins or 29 ... Nxe6 30 Bxh7+! wins) 29 ... Rd8 30 Bg5 resigns.

The thrust of White's attack initiated by 23 e5 and followed up with a series of hammer-blows, lasted only 7 moves, but what great effect they had.

Moral. When the position calls for attack, do so with vigour, precision and without compromise, by using each piece to its maximum effect.

6. *Kopec–N. Ocipoff, Pan-American Intercollegiate, Louisville, Kentucky, 1974 (Dartmouth College vs. City College New York)*

If you're looking for an immediate finish through the queen sacrifice 21 dxc6 Rxd2 22 Rxd2 etc., you're on the right track, though a bit premature. First it is better to prise open the lines to the black king from the sniper tactics started by 21 h5. Play continued: 21 ... Ne7 (attacking the d-pawn and guarding g6) 22 Nh4! (the only consistent move as 22 d6 Nf5 23 Bxf5 gxf5 leaves White's d-pawn weak with no counterplay. Since that pawn must fall in any case, White adds pressure to the weak-est point in Black's position) 22 ... Rxd5 (see Diagram 6a).

6a. *Kopec–Ocipoff (after 22 ... Rxd5 23 hxg6+ fxg6)*

The position requires such precision as to merit another diagram. There is only one convincing and winning move, e.g. 24 Bxg6+?! Nxg6 25 Qxd5 Qxh4 and 24 Nxg6? Rxd2 25 Nxf8+ Kg8 etc. are both inadequate. Necessary is 24 Qxd5!! forcing the black knight away from its defence of g6. Play continued: 24 ... Nxd5 25 Nxg6 (with the primary threats 26 Nxf8+ and 26 Rxd5) 25 ... Bb7 (perhaps the best try was 25 ... Qa8) 26 Nxf8+ Kg8 27 Ne6 Qf6 28 Nxg7 Kxg7 29 Be4 Qf7 (on 29 ... Nxe3 Rd7+ and 31 Rxb7 +−) 30 Bxd5 Bxd5 31 Rc3 (Black has no answer to this rook doubling manoeuvre) 31 ... Qb7 32 Rdc1 Qa6 33 Rc7+ Kg6 34 Rd7 Qd3 35 Rd6+ Kf5 36 Rxh6 a5 37 Rc8 Qb1+ 38 Kh2 Qxa2 39 Rxb6 Qe2 40 Rh8 Qf1 41 f3 e4 42 g4+ (42 Rh5 is mate, but both sides were in time trouble) 42 ... Ke5 43 Rh5 mate.

Moral. Once you set upon a strategical theme (21 h5 and the weakening of g6) see it through to its logical conclusion with the tactics necessary to support it.

EXERCISES II: Lessons 9–12. How to Formulate a Plan

In the exercises which follow there is not necessarily just one "good" plan and you need not exhaust yourself poring over precise lines. Instead, study the positions going through the four-point mental process outlined in the introduction to Lessons 9–12, namely: (1) Assessment, (2) Objective, (3) Plan, (4) Method of execution.

Having identified what you consider to be the essential features of the position, the solution can then be studied and learned from. Remember that top grandmasters thought for a long time in several of the positions, so don't be discouraged if you do not spot every trick and nuance.

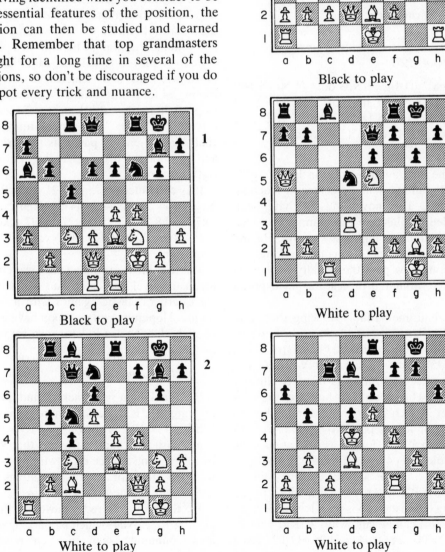

3

Black to play

1

Black to play

2

White to play

4

White to play

5

White to play

111

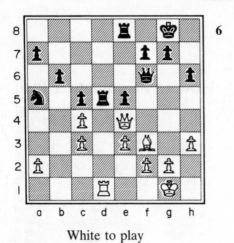

White to play

How to Formulate a Plan

1. *Penrose–Keene, British Championship, Blackpool, 1971*

(1 e4 g6 2 d4 Bg7 3 Nc3 d6 4 f4 Nf6 5 Nf3 0–0 6 Bd3 Nc6 7 h3 Nb4 8 Be3 b6 9 a3 Nxd3+ 10 cxd3 c5 11 Qd2 Ba6 12 Kf2? Rc8 13 Rhc1 Nd7 14 d5 e6 15 dxe6 fxe6 16 Re1? Nf6 17 Rad1?)

In the diagrammed position Black's plan of undermining White's centre is reaching its climax. The moves thus far have been provided to illustrate the manner in which White built up an impressive centre. Having considered but not executed a king-side attack, he now pays the penalty for having badly co-ordinated pieces and an exposed king.

The half-open f-file menacing the white king, Black's well-placed pieces, bishop pair and mobile centre allowed him to strike with 17 ... d5! Now we see that White's "impressive" centralization is of mere illusory strength. His pieces are huddled together and get in each other's way, forcing him to capture or lose a piece to ... d4. After 18 exd5 exd5 19 d4 (forced as before but now the "hole" on e4 leads to further opening of lines) 19 ... Ne4+ 20 Nxe4 dxe4 21 Ne5 g5! (and now Black proves that White's proud looking outpost on e5 is merely transient, as its support can be cut away) 22 Kg1 gxf4 23 Bxf4 Qxd4+ 24 Qxd4 cxd4 25 g3 (if 25 Rxe4

then 25 ... Rxf4 26 Rxf4 Bxe5 wins) 25 ... Rfe8 26 Rxe4 Rc5 27 Rde1 d3 and the combination of Black's passed d-pawn, raking bishops and well-placed rooks left White totally lost.

The game finished: 28 Nf3 Rxe4 29 Rxe4 Bb7 30 Re3 d2 31 Nxd2 Bd4 32 Kf1 Ba6+ 33 Kg2 Bxe3 34 Bxe3 Rc2 35 b3 Bb7+ 36 Kf1 Bd5 37 Ke1 Bxb3! White resigned. (If 38 Nxb3 Rc3 wins.)

2. *Penrose–Tal, Leipzig 1960*

White has a powerful attacking position but must now find the best way to press home his advantage. Direct attack is called for, but an immediate f5 would give Black the beautiful square e5 for his knight and allow him to disentangle his cramped pieces.

Penrose played 19 e5! dxe5 20 f5! and the pawn sacrifice had sealed off e5 while freeing e4 for White's knights, allowing him to press home his attack on the f-file. The square e4 is an "effective outpost", as challenge by enemy pawns is not practical and it undoubtedly passes the usefulness test!

Play continued 20 ... Bb7 21 Rad1 Ba8 22 Nce4 Na4 23 Bxa4 bxa4 24 fxg6 fxg6 25 Qf7+ Kh8 26 Nc5 Qa7 27 Qxd7 Qxd7 28 Nxd7 Rxb2 29 Nb6 Rb3 30 Nxc4 and White soon won.

White's idea in this game was by no means a novel one as he had undoubtedly seen earlier "classic" games with a similar theme. Hopefully you will soon have a store of such ideas to use in your own games.

3. *McNab–Sowray, Phillip & Drew "Knights", London 1982*

Black's knight is attacked and his immediate task is to decide where to move it. While 10 ... Ne7 is obvious and reasonable, Black wished to exploit the fact that White, by recapturing a piece on f3 with his g-pawn to open files for a possible attack, had seriously weakened the square f4.

He therefore offered a pawn sacrifice by playing 10 ... Nd4! which is, once again, an idea commonly seen in such positions.

White accepted the offer and play continued 11 Bxd4 exd4 12 Qxd4 Nh5. Now the full point of Black's plan is clear. Not only will his knight reach f4, where it will be aggressively placed, but he also controls all the central dark squares with his bishop and queen. Squares such as e5, g5, h4 and h6 can be used to deploy these pieces and cement Black's grip. In the play which follows White's pieces are suffocated by his immobile pawns.

The game continued: 13 Qc4 Nf4 14 Bf1 a6 15 Qb3 Qg5 16 Ne2 Bh6 (note how White's king is now caught in the centre on the potentially dangerous half-open e-file, in addition to his other problems) 17 Rg1 Qe5 18 Qc3 Qe7 19 Rg4 Nxe2 20 Bxe2 Rae8 21 Qd3 Qe5 22 c3 Qh2 23 Kd1 f5 24 exf5 Qh1+ 25 Bf1 Rxf5 26 Rg3 Ref8 27 Kc2 Rxf3 28 Rxf3 Qxf3 29 Qxf3 Rxf3 30 Kb3 Rxf2 and Black was winning.

The game ending decisively after 58 moves in a win . . . for White! Black's bishop became the pathetically bad piece which featured in the endgame diagram on page 62. Sadists among you may care to refresh your memories!

4. *Kasparov–Petrosian, Bugojno 1982*

White obviously has a clear advantage with his rooks well placed on open files, a powerful bishop on the h1→a8 diagonal, an active queen and a well-placed knight which can be dislodged only by the weakening move ... f6. Black, on the other hand, is seriously behind in development and will be struggling to find any way of developing his bishop and thereafter co-ordinating his rooks. He has also played ... g6 weakening his king-side dark squares. White's objective must be to maintain his bind on the position, while seeking a way to penetrate on the open files and gain a more tangible advantage.

Petrosian's one well-placed piece is the knight on d5, which guards the entry square at c7, while blocking the d-file. Accordingly, Kasparov dislodges it, but not by the obvious 18 Bxd5? exd5 19 Qxd5 Be6 when

Black obtains some counterplay. Instead he played 18 e4! (trading in the long diagonal to maintain his bind and break through on the open files) 18 ... Nb6 (still blocking the road to c7) 19 Bf1! (a subtle move, reactivating the bishop and preparing the tactics which arise shortly) 19 ... Re8 20 Rdd1 Rf8 (Black is totally tied up — he cannot play a piece to d7 because of Rc7) 21 a3 Kg7 22 b3 Kg8 23 a4 Rd8 24 Qc5! (The point! As soon as Black tries to contest the d-file, White forces a neat tactical win, for example if:

(a) 24 ... Qxc5 25 Rxd8+ Qf8 26 Rxf8+ Kxf8 27 Rc7 with the devastating twin threats of 28 Rxf7+ and 28 a5 trapping the knight! Or if
(b) 24 ... Qf8 25 Qxf8+ Rxf8 26 a5 or
(c) 24 ... Qe8 25 Ng4.)

Black resigned!

A fine example of how to cash in an advantage while giving your opponent no chance to fight back. Should you not have seen everything, do not despair; at the time Kasparov nominated this as the best game he'd ever played!

5. *Tarrasch–Teichmann, San Sebastian 1912*

Once again White stands clearly better, the most striking feature of the position being his well-placed king on d4. The king ties a black rook to the c-file to guard against its further penetration and means that Black must avoid excessive liquidation as this would almost certainly lead to a lost endgame. Furthermore, Black's pawn structure is the more cramped and his bad bishop has little scope, whereas White has excellent communications between the two wings and the centre of his position, giving his pieces greater mobility.

Nevertheless, Black is not about to lie down and die and White must find a plan which will force the issue. Tarrasch achieved this, overstretching Black by launching a king-side attack which opened files thereby enabling the infiltration of Black's weakened pawn shield. He continued 26 g4 Bc8 27 h4. This threatens 28 g5 h5 29 g6 and the black h-pawn is doomed. Black is thus forced to make further king-side pawn moves and must have bitterly regretted playing 22 ... h6 which weakened his pawns and greatly accelerated the speed at which White could force open files. This is a typical example of why one should avoid casual pawn moves needlessly creating weaknesses for your opponent to attack.

The game finished: 27 ... g6 28 Rh1 Kg7 29 h5 Rh8 30 Rfh2 Bd7 31 g5 (forcing open lines) 31 ... hxg5 32 fxg5 gxh5 33 Rxh5 Rxh5 34 Rxh5 Kf8 35 Rh8+ Ke7 36 g6 fxg6 37 Bxg6 b4 38 Rh7+ Kd8 39 Bd3 Rc3 40 a3 a5 41 Rh8+ Ke7 42 Ra8 and Black resigned — his queen-side pawns are doomed as his position has been outflanked.

6.*Botvinnik–Chekhover, Leningrad 1938*

There are often many factors to be considered in assessing a position. In the diagrammed position Black has only two pawn islands as against White's three, while White's doubled, isolated c-pawns look rather sick. Black has just captured a rook on d5 and the automatic "structural" recapture is 21 cxd5 creating a protected passed pawn. Pieces, not just pawns, must be considered however and White's active, centralized queen, rook and bishop give scope for dynamic play, exploiting open lines.

Botvinnik avoided 21 cxd5 because of 21 ... Qd6 blockading the passed pawn and making progress difficult. He played 21 Rxd5!! preserving his grip on the d-file (21 ... Rd8 loses to 22 Rxe5 as 22 ... Nxc4 loses a piece after 23 Re8+ Rxe8 24 Qxe8+ Kh7 25 Qe4+). The remainder of the game is instructive for the impressive blend of tactics and positional themes which Botvinnik employs to seize the 7th rank and establish an iron grip on the position.

Play continued 21 ... Qe7 22 Bg4! Qb7 23 Bf5 Qb8 24 Rd7 Rd8 25 Qxe5! Nxc4 26 Qxb8 Rxb8 27 Be4! (White rejects 27 Rxa7 in favour of increasing his positional grip) 27 ... Na3 28 Bd5 Rf8 29 e4 a5 30 c4 b5 31 cxb5 Nxb5 32 e5 a4 33 f4! (envisaging a powerful passed e-pawn) 33 ... Nd4 34 Kf2 g5 35 g3 gxf4 36 gxf4 Ne6 37 Ke3 c4 38 f5 Nc5 39 Rc7 Nd3 40 e6 fxe6 41 fxe6 and Black resigned.

Winning chess often requires flexible thinking in order that the key themes in a particular position may be recognized.

EXERCISES III: Lessons 13–16. Opening Principles and Ideas

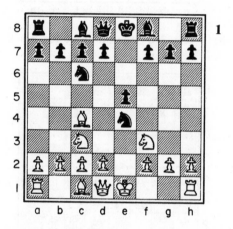

(1) Does 5 Bxf7+ give Black serious headaches?

(3) What should Black to move play?

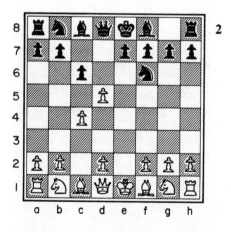

(2) Could and should White play to win a pawn?

(4) Does Black to move need to retreat?

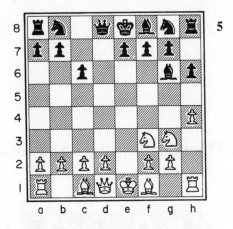

(5)· What should White to move play?

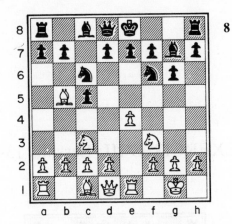

(8) Is 6 … Nd4 a good move for Black?

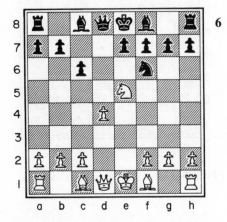

(6) Black to play. What is the number one priority?

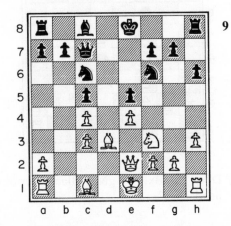

(9) Why did White play the odd-looking 12 Nh2?

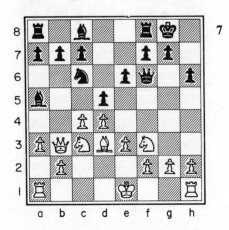

(7) White's king is uncastled. Can Black to play exploit this factor?

(10) Black to play is threatened by 10 Bg5. What is the best move?

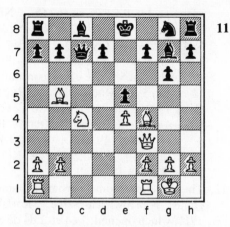

(11) How does White to play deny Black the time needed to complete development?

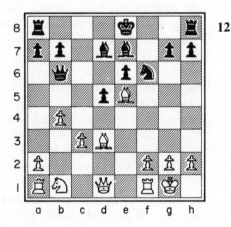

(12) Of the moves 13 Nd2 and 13 Qc2, which is better and why?

Opening Principles and Ideas

1. Not at all. After 5 ... Kxf7 6 Nxe4 d5, Black's powerful centre and smooth development more than compensate for the slight inconvenience to the king.

2. White could but shouldn't. After 4 dxc6 Nxc6, Black could play ... e5 and ... Bc5 with beautiful development and a powerful central outpost at d4.

3. Above all Black shouldn't allow the heartbreaking threat of 6 Nd6 mate. 5 ... Ndf6 is a simple way of making White's queen look rather stupid on e2.

4. Certainly not! 7 ... d5! is both thematic and strong when 8 exf6 dxc4 9 Re1+ Be6 leaves Black with an excellent game.

5. This position arose after the moves: 1 e4 c6 2 Nc3 d5 3 Nf3 dxe4 4 Nxe4 Bf5? 5 Ng3 Bg6 6 h4 h6, and illustrates an instructive opening mistake. 4 ... Bf5 5 Ng3 Bg6 is fine after 1 e4 c6 2 d4 d5 3 Nc3 dxe4 4 Nxe4 but not here. White has the powerful centralization 7 Ne5! A game Alekhine–Bruce, Plymouth 1938, continued: 7 ... Bh7 8 Qh5! g6 9 Bc4! e6 10 Qe2 Nf6 11 Nxf7 Kxf7 12 Qxe6+ 1–0 whilst Alekhine–Navarro, Madrid 1940, went 7 ... Nd7 8 Nxg6 fxg6 9 d4 e5 10 Qg4 Qf6 11 Be3 Ne7 12 Ne4 1–0.

6. The main goal should be to get rid of White's powerfully centralized knight and to this end the retrograde 7 ... Nd7! is extremely logical. Before the discovery of 7 ... Nd7! Black had been destroyed several times in the variation 7 ... Bf5 8 g4 Be4 9 f3 Bg6 10 h4! Whilst 7 ... Be6 had left him passively placed in lines such as 8 Be2 g6 9 0–0 Bg7 10 c4 0–0 11 Be3.

7. This position, taken from a game Fish–Abrahams, Liverpool 1929, came about after the moves 1 d4 Nf6 2 c4 e6 3 Nf3 d5 4 Bg5 h6 5 Bxf6 Qxf6 6 Nc3 Bb4 7 Qb3 Nc6 8 a3 Ba5 9 e3 0–0 10 Bd3. Abrahams exploited White's uncastled king with the ingenious stroke 10 ... e5! The astonishing sequel was 11 cxd5 exd4 12 exd4 Re8+ 13 Kf1 Qxcf3!! 14 gxf3 Bh3+ 15 Kg1 Nxd4 16 Qd1 Re1+! 17 Qxe1 Nxf3 mate.

8. No. It moves a piece twice in the opening and constitutes a premature attempt to seize the initiative. Rosso-limo–Romanenko, Salzburg 1948, continued 6 ... Nd4? (better is 6 ... 0–0) 7 e5! Ng8 (If 7 ... Nxb5? 8 exf6 Nxc3 9 fxg7+–) 8 d3 Nxb5 9 Nxb5 a6 10 Nd6+!! exd6 11 Bg5! Qa5 12 exd6+ Kf8 13 Re8+!! Kxe8 14 Qe2+ Kf8 15 Be7+ Ke8 16 Bd8+!! Kxd8 17 Ng5 1–0.

9. The position arose in a game Keene–Ligterink, London 1981. Keene's knight is en route for the square d5 via h2, f1 and e3. After 12 Nh2! b6 13 Nf1 Ba6 14 Ne3 0-0-0 15 Nd5 the knight had become a monster!

10. The position is taken from a game Botvinnik–Reshevsky, World Championship Tournament 1948. 9 ... h6 is obvious yet dubious as Black would thereby weaken his kingside. Reshevsky played 9 ... Ne8!, an apparently retrograde action but one which contains several subtle ideas:

(a) The pin 10 Bg5 is prevented.
(b) A subsequent f4 by White can be paried by ... f5.
(c) Black's knight could at some stage go to d6 where it would help gang up on the weak c4 pawn.

The continuation of Botvinnik–Reshevsky was highly instructive: 10 0-0 Ba6 11 Be3 d6 12 Ng3 Na5 13 Qe2 Qd7 14 f4? (14 e5!) 14 ... f5 15 Rae1 g6 16 Rd1 Qf7 17 e5 Rc8 18 Rfe1 dxe5 19 dxe5 Ng7 20 Nf1 Rfd8 21 Bf2 Nh5 22 Bg3 Qe8 23 Ne3 Qa4 24 Qa2 Nxg3 25 hxg3 h5 26 Be2 Kf7 27 Kf2 Qb3 28 Qxb3 Nxb3 29 Bd3 Ke7 30 Ke2 Na5 31 Rd2 Rc7 32 g4 Rcd7 33 gxf5 gxf5 34 Red1 h4 35 Ke1 Nb3 36 Nd5+ exd5 37 Bxf5 Nxd2 38 Rxd2 dxc4 39 Bxd7 Rxd7 40 Rf2 Ke6 41 Rf3 Rd3 42 Ke2 0-1.

11. The diagrammed position is Rossolimo–O'Kelly, Oldenburg 1949, and arose after the moves: 1 e4 c5 2 Nf3 Nc6 3 Bb5 g6 4 0-0 Bg7 5 c3 e6? (5 ... Nf6!) 6 d4 cxd4 7 cxd4 Qb6? 8 Na3 Nxd4 9 Nc4! Nxf3+ 10 Qxf3 Qc7 11 Bf4 e5. Rossolimo now produced the brilliant stroke 12 Nxe5!!, the game continuing: 12 ... Bxe5 13 Rac1 Qb8 14 Rxc8+! Qxc8 15 Bxe5 f6 16 Bxf6 Nxf6 17 Qxf6 Rf8 18 Qe5+ (18 Qe6+! Kd8 19 Rd1 +−) 18 ... Kd8 19 Qg5+ Ke8 20 Rc1 Qd8 21 Qe5+ Qe7 22 Bxd7+ Kf7 23 Be6+ Ke8 24 Rc7 1-0.

12. The position comes from a famous game Nimzowitsch–Salve, Karlsbad 1911, which opened: 1 e4 e6 2 d4 d5 3 e5 c5 4 c3 Nc6 5 Nf3 Qb6 6 Bd3 Bd7 7 dxc5 Bxc5 8 0-0 f6 9 b4 Be7 10 Bf4 fxe5 11 Nxe5 Nxe5 12 Bxe5 Nf6.

The apparently strong 13 Qc2 does not conform to the essential requirements of controlling the central squares d4 and e5. Black could sacrifice a pawn by 13 ... 0-0 14 Bxf6 Bxf6 15 Bxh7+ Kh8, when his centre pawns would become mobile and dangerous. Nimzowitsch did not allow himself to be distracted in such a way and played a beautifully thematic game: 13 Nd2! 0-0 14 Nf3 Bd6 15 Qe2! Rac8 16 Bd4 Qc7 17 Ne5 Be8 18 Rae1 Bxe5 19 Bxe5 Qc6 20 Bd4 Bd7 21 Qc2 Rf7 22 Re3 b6 23 Rg3 Kh8 24 Bxh7! e5 (too little, too late) 25 Bg6 Re7 26 Re1 Qd6 27 Be3 d4 28 Bg5 Rxc3 29 Rxc3 dxc3 30 Qxc3 Kg8 31 a3 Kf8 32 Bh4 Be8 33 Bf5 Qd4 34 Qxd4 exd4 35 Rxe7 Kxe7 36 Bd3 Kd6 37 Bxf6 gxf6 38 h4 1-0.

EXERCISES IV: Lessons 17–21. Endings

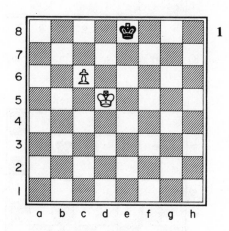

(1) White to play and win.

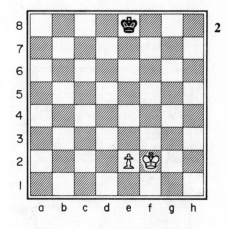

(2) White to play. What result?

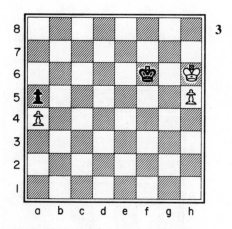

(3) White to play. What result?

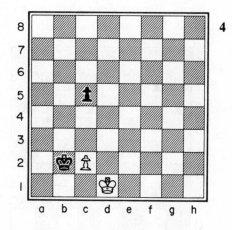

(4) White to play and draw.

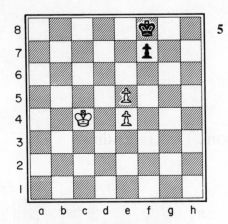

(5) White to play and win.

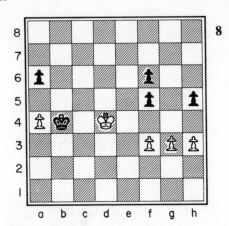

(8) What result with White to play?

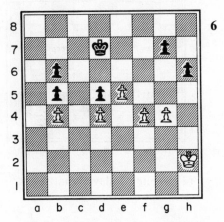

(6) Black's position looks hopeless, yet White offered a draw after Black's next move. What was it?

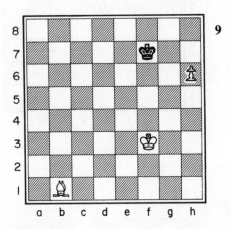

(9) White to play. What result?

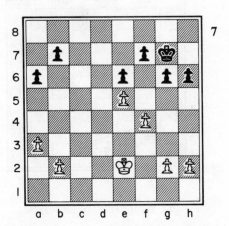

(7) Tartakower, playing against Schlechter, produced 1 ... g5? here. That was a bad mistake — can you see why? What, then, is White's winning plan?

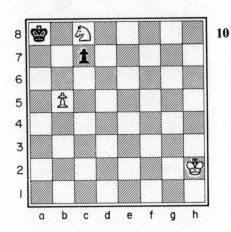

(10) White to play and win.

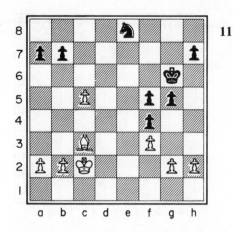

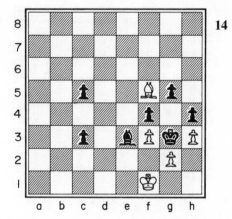

(11) White (Fischer) plays a good move.

(14) Black is two pawns up, but with bishops of opposite colour the win still seems far off. Black to play and win.

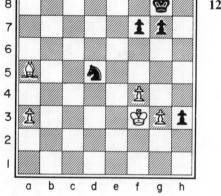

'12) Black (Tal) plays a good move also.

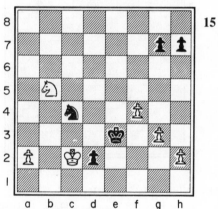

(15) Black to play and win.

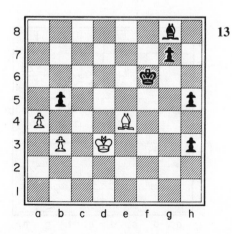

(13) A study by Rinck. White to play and win in very instructive fashion.

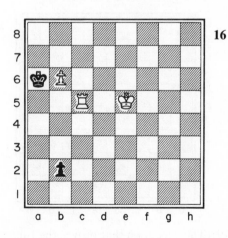

(16) A study by Lolli. White to play and win.

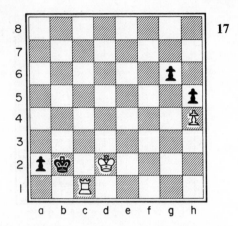

(17) A trick worth knowing. White to play.

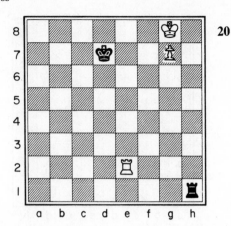

(20) You should know this one by now. White to play.

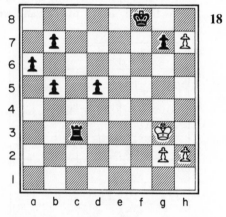

(18) White played 1 Kg4? here and that cost him the game. How did Black then manage to stop the h-pawn?

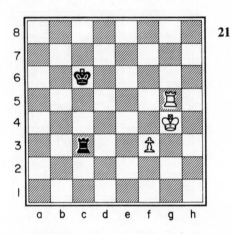

(21) Tal (White) made another good move here.

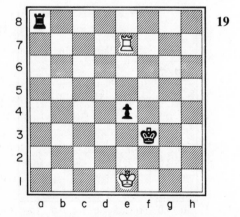

(19) The exception that proves the rule and that a little learning can be a dangerous thing. White to play and draw.

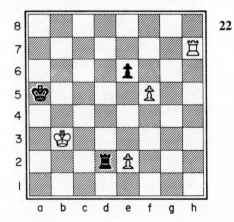

(22) Rinck again. White plays and wins in style.

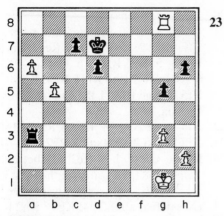

23

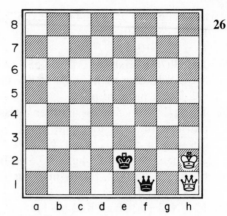

26

(23) White is in a position to make use of a common theme in rook and pawn endings.

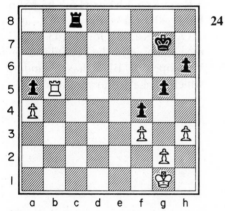

24

(24) What is Black's best move here and how would you rate the chances of survival?

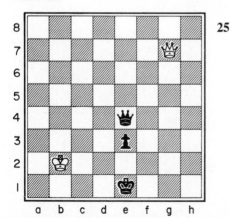

25

(25) Black had struggled on for many hours to reach the diagrammed position and now came up with 1 ... e2. What happened next?

(26) Black sealed 1 ... Qf4+ here and had to face the wrath of "some bystanders who audibly criticized her for trying to win such an obviously drawn position". She then agreed to a draw. Would you?!

Endings

1. 1 Ke6! (opposition!). 1 Kc5 also wins, but not 1 Kd6??(=).
2. 1 Ke3 Ke7 2 Ke4 Ke6 3 e3! and the spare pawn move is decisive (1–0).
3. 1 Kh7 Kf7 2 h6 Kf8 3 Kg6 Kg8 4 Kf6 Kh7 5 Ke6 Kxh6 6 Kd6 Kg7 7 Kc6 Kf7 8 Kb5 Ke7 9 Kxa5 Kd7 10 Kb6 Kc8 and Black draws by a hair's breadth. Simple counting can be important in king plus pawn endings. Black never reached this "might-have-been", choosing to resign earlier.
4. 1 c4!
5. 1 e6!! fxe6 2 e5!
6. 1 ... g5! and the White king has no way through.
7. 1 ... g5? allowed White to create a D.P.P. after 2 fxg5 hxg5 3 Kf3 Kg6 4 Kg4 f5+ 5 exf6 Kxf6 6 g3! a5 7 a4 e5 8 h4 and wins.
8. 1 h4!! followed by the breakthrough g4 is decisive (1–0).
9. 1 Bh7! keeps the black king out of the corner and wins (1 ... Kf6 2 Kf4).
10. 1 Nb6+!! (pawn on 5th vs. pawn on 6th).
11. 1 Be5! cornered the black knight and there followed 1 ... Kh5 2 Kd3 g4 3 b4

a6 4 a4 gxf3 5 gxf3 Kh4 6 b5 axb5 7 a5!
Kh3 8 c6! (1–0).

12. 1 ... Ne3! (0–1).

13. 1 a5 Bh7(!) 2 Bxh7 g6 3 Bg8 Ke5 4 a6 h2
5 Bd5!! Kxd5 6 a7 h1(=Q) 7 a8(=Q)+
is a lovely piece of play.

14. 1 ... g4! (to create another passed
pawn) is the only idea and Black went
on to win after 2 hxg4 (2 fxg4 f3!)
2 ... h3! 3 gxh3 Kxf3 4 g5 Kg3 5 g6 Bd4
6 h4 f3! 7 h5 Bg7, finally manoeuvring
his king to d2.

15. 1 ... Na3+! 2 Nxa3 Ke2 (0–1).

16. 1 Rb5! Kxb5 2 b7 (1–0).

17. 1 Ra1!! Kxa1 2 Kc2 (1–0).

18. 1 Kg4? Rc4+ 2 Kg5 Rh4!! 3 Kxh4 g5+!
(0–1).

19. A difficult one. White played 1 Rf7+?
Ke3 2 Kf1 Ra1+ 3 Kg2 Kd3 4 Rd7+
Ke2 5 Rb7 e3 6 Rb8 Kd2 and lost. The
idea (of going to the "shorter side") was
right, but the first priority here is to stop
the pawn's advance. 1 Kd2! draws
(1 ... Ra2+ 2 Ke1 Ke3 3 Kf1! Kd3 4
Re8! Ra1+ 5 Kf2).

20. 1 Re4! (Lucena).

21. 1 Re5! cuts off the king and wins after
1 ... Kd6 2 Re8 Kd7 3 Re1 Rc8 4 f4
Rg8+ 5 Kf5 Rf8+ 6 Kg5 (1–0). On
6 ... Rg8+ 7 Kh6 Rf8 8 Re4! Kd6 9 Kg7
Rf5 10 Kg6 Rf8 11 f5 heads towards the
Lucena.

22. 1 f6 Rxe2 2 Rh5+ Kb6 3 Rf5!! (1–0).

23. 1 b6! cxb6 2 a7 Rxa7 3 Rg7+ (1–0).

24. If you chose 1 ... Rc2 or, better still
1 ... Rc1+ then you have the right idea.
1 ... Ra8? is unnecessarily passive and
risks defeat after 2 h4! Kg6 3 Kh2 Ra7 4
Kh3 Kh5 5 hxg5 hxg5 6 g3! fxg3 7 f4. On
principle, Black should try to keep the
rook active, and 1 ... Rc1+ 2 Kh2 Ra1
3 Rxa5 Kg6 4 h4 gxh4 5 Kh3 h5! 6 Kh2
h3! 7 gxh3 Ra2+ draws with ease.

25. 1 Qg1+ Kd2 2 Qc1+ Kd3 3 Qc3 is a
nice example of the "epaulette" mate.

26. We hope not. Black has a standard win
which we have shown already.

Lesson 21

PRACTICAL TOURNAMENT TIPS AND ADVICE

IAN D. MULLEN and others

This last section is written in an attempt to bridge the yawning gap which so often can separate theory from practice. We, the authors, hope that you have enjoyed what you have read so far and trust that much of it will be of use in the field of combat. Anyone who understands fully only a quarter of what is contained here knows a lot; but there are still a few points which require mention.

Chess, by its very nature, is a very competitive game. To some it may be an art form, and in many ways it can resemble a science; but anyone who has tasted the experience of real tournament play knows that, in essence, a game of chess is a BATTLE — where the stronger (and/or luckier) player emerges victorious. As a parting shot we will mention that, for humans, psychology, attitude and nerves are as much a part of the game as anything else. This book is not written for computers, so we thought it wise to include a few ideas on how to survive in the chessboard jungle. Here are a few practical suggestions which might tie up a few loose ends.

(1) *Time is precious* and its use and abuse varies immensely from player to player. It does not matter how good your position looks when you lose on time; the score on the notice board will still tell the same sad story: no points. The clock is an integral part of the modern game and there is only one real cure for time trouble — don't take so long over your moves! It makes good sense to advise the novice to try to "stagger" his game; e.g. when playing a time control of 40 moves per 2 hours, play the first 10 moves in something under 30 minutes, and the first 20 in something around an hour — which is to say, keep one eye on the clock.

Efficient use of thinking time in chess can make a big difference to any player's results. Three common causes of unnecessary time trouble are:

(a) Where there is a choice of equally plausible looking moves and the player feels that he cannot choose between them.

(b) Where the player has decided which move to make next but still insists on checking and rechecking the consequences.

(c) Daydreaming (or perhaps stage-fright).

If you cannot make up your mind which move to play next then try to make a rational choice but don't waste time striving for perfection. If you do know which move you are going to play, then PLAY IT and leave your opponent to work out the consequences. If you like daydreaming or just get a plain thrill from being in time trouble, then enjoy it; but don't complain when your flag falls. Kotov has suggested that you make use of your opponent's time by looking at the position from your opponent's point of view while it is his turn to move. Also, to concentrate on the strategical and long term possibilities on the board. Many players simply waste their opponent's thinking time.

It is a good idea to try to recognize when the critical or turning point of a game is approaching. What is sometimes worse than wasting time is to play too quickly when the position on the board demands a deep think. If you feel there is something "on", then trust your instinct and try to find it. It is very common to see a player take 20 or so minutes over a critical move and then the

125

position clarifies and the following moves become easier. If you play quickly and superficially in a complicated situation (as many inexperienced players do) you are likely to miss something you will regret. By the way, if your opponent insists on circling the numbers 30 to 40 on his scoresheet before the game has started then be prepared. Most players underline move 40 (or the relevant time control) at the start of a game — just in case. The best advice we can offer you when facing an opponent who is left with 10 moves to make in a minute is to ignore it. Your opponent will be nervous with a good position, and desperate with a bad one. Either way, you can compound your adversary's problems and relax your own nerves by taking a "time out". If your own position happens to be near hopeless it might be worth trying the "blitz" technique. Blast out your moves as quickly as possible and hope for a blunder.

Allegro finishes can be a nightmare for some people. Five-minute chess is looked down upon in certain circles, but it can prove a handy preparation for this nerve wracking situation. Often it is psychologically difficult to readjust to having to move quickly after a long, hard struggle. This has proved to be the downfall of many a good, but slow player. The only recommendation we can offer is to let yourself go and treat the allegro finish as no more than a glorified 5-minute game (bearing in mind the difference in rules, touch move etc.).

(2) *Nerves.*

"Under no circumstances should one become nervous, because nervousness consumes energy. One must continually remember that all this is not so terribly important, that the result of a chess tournament is not a matter of life and death."

A fine piece of advice from Nimzowitsch, though we admit that this comes from the same man who reputedly leapt on to a chess table after an unexpected defeat and screamed: "Why must I lose to this idiot!"

Karpov, particularly, has emphasized the importance of strong nerves for success in chess and he is one person who should know. Every chess player has two basic fears to overcome: the fear of losing, and what is sometimes worse, the fear of winning! On this topic, Nimzowitsch preached the use of what would nowadays be called meditation; i.e. occasionally clear your mind of all thoughts and relax — something which is hard to achieve, but is worth trying. This, and similar methods can also be profitably employed to soothe jangling nerves before an important game. Other obvious suggestions are to walk out the adrenalin and knock back a cup of (mild) coffee, or perhaps (à la Miles) milk.

A healthy flow of adrenalin is a useful thing in most competitive situations and if you are wise enough not to take the game too seriously there should be no problem in this direction; but remember, with no tension, there would be no game.

(3) *Winning chess* has a lot to do with playing good moves, but it has more to do with not playing bad ones. If you play 10 excellent moves, 10 average ones and then a lulu, there is every likelihood that your opponent may still win without having played as well as you for 90% of the game. A basic requisite for improvement in chess is an avoidance of blunders. One tried and trusted method is to write down the move before you play it and then to check to see if you are about to leave a mate in one on the board. A well-known Scottish player took this idea a step further and developed a system of writing indecipherable scrawls on his scoresheet before making his move — he was mentally (and physically) ticking off a series of questions directed to himself: "Does my opponent have a check?"; "Can I be forked?"; "Is there a surprise move I have overlooked?", etc. It worked! (Although this is strictly illegal since no form of notetaking is allowed during a chess game other than a record of the moves.) The main distinguishing mark of the 2200 player is often not so much the brilliance of his play,

but the wonderful lack of unforced errors.

(4) *Making your move*. Danny Kopec has already touched on this subject in his section, but some points are worth repeating. *Think Like a Grandmaster* has been one of the most influential chess books of its time and in it Kotov offered the following valuable piece of advice on systematic and efficient decision making. When in the process of choosing which move to play, first of all sift through all the "candidate moves" (all the potentially good moves you can see in the position). Go through them one by one, carefully analysing each possibility as well as you are able; then make your choice. If you have developed some faith in your analytical ability, you will not need to continually recheck the variations. Any method of semi-organized thinking is generally more efficient than a mystical groping for inspiration from the heavens above. Here is an insight into the mind's eye of a chess player at work:

> "O.K. I can play e5 now, that looks nice. Hmmmm, maybe h3 and drive his knight away first. What else? Any other moves? Re1 Nc3. Just develop? Maybe. Anything else? No . . . WAIT. What about b4 for a laugh? I don't think so. Right, that's the lot.
> e5, h3, Re1, or Nc3. That's the choice . . . e5 first.
> O.K. e5, then he plays d5, maybe d6. So e5, d5, then I play, then he plays, then I play, etc.

This beautifully simple idea of trying to put some order into the normally chaotic thought process of the chess player is one of the best pieces of advice I have ever read in a chess book. Properly applied, practised and perfected, this can lift you from the murky haze to something approaching clarity in thought!

(5) *Developing a style*. Everyone has his own particular preferences as to what types of position he enjoys playing, and also a personal bias in the choice of chess "heroes" and "villains". To some, Petrosian is a name which conjures up visions of fianchettoed bishops, exasperating manoeuvring and lots of draws; to others, his play is like a dream. I once asked Jon Speelman on how to improve at chess and the most tangible reply he gave me was to pick a model — some famous player whose games I enjoyed and with whose style I felt an empathy. I chose Fischer, and he replied, (somewhat enigmatically): "Ah, Fischer has a very complicated style." He suggested I pick a less unattainable goal and base my play round that — steal his opening repertoire, fathom his ideas and generally try to become a mini whoever-it-was. This is certainly a clever (if not original) idea and labour-saving device; a do-it-yourself ready-made style. But do you really know your own style?

(6) *Know thyself* and try to become aware of your own strengths and weaknesses. Pick an opening which suits your temperament and aim for positions you enjoy playing. An even position which one player enjoys playing, and the other doesn't, is not an even position! Don't be afraid to play a move which isn't in the books; a lot of what is in the books is wrong anyway. Try not to let the grading list intimidate you too much. If you are paired against a player who, on paper, is far stronger than yourself, you will not cause worry by keeping your pieces in your own half of the board and playing for a draw. In such situations the only practical policy is to put aside your inhibitions and have a go. You may not win, but at least you will make a game of it. As far as your pieces are concerned, "when in doubt, get them out". Also, "the threat is stronger than the execution" (Nimzowitsch); i.e. errors are far more likely to occur when a player has a wide choice of moves than when forced into playing good moves by the opponent's threats. "Give someone enough rope and they will hang themselves" is often the philosophy strong players apply when playing rabbits. Most players will occasionally vary their openings to suit a particular opponent and the psychological battle fought in the first few moves is often an

important one. Contrary to popular opinion, many strong players are not walking memory machines and they also know less opening theory than some would suppose; but what they do know, they know well and certainly know how to put into practice. (Refer to lesson 15, Opening Principles and Ideas.)

(7) *Health*. When asked what he thought was the most important asset for success in chess, Fischer mentioned that top of his personal list was health. Botvinnik made a point of going for an hour's walk every day during a tournament and every chess player must pay a certain amount of attention to general fitness for the brain to function at anywhere near peak capacity. On the other side of the coin, Timman once told of an episode when he prepared for a major tournament by retreating to the country, carefully watching his diet, and religiously setting out for daily training runs. Later, he bemoaned the fact that when he sat down at the board, his by then rippling torso was bursting with so much energy that he could not retain his concentration and, as a result, played badly. Timman sensibly recommends that you stick to your normal routine when playing in a tournament. However, he is a professional, and it is not within most players' normal routine to face five hard games of chess in the space of three days (at a weekend tournament) without suffering from some form of fatigue. Walking is nature's tranquillizer — exertion without exhaustion — a brisk stroll before a game can do nothing but good for the body and brain. Also, it normally makes good sense to avoid eating a big meal before a game, for fairly obvious reasons (though, as if to be awkward, we have heard it said that Larsen enjoys a hefty meal before he plays and says it calms down his over-active mind). You don't need to go to the length of juggling with medicine balls but a 5-hour playing session will be pretty exhausting if you are in no way prepared for it.

(8) *Post mortems*. You can learn more from your losses than your wins. Make a point of analysing your games and pinpointing your errors — especially the typical ones which you notice recurring time and time again. Try to get a stronger player to go over your games with you and do not be afraid to ask the said stronger player about pieces of analysis or openings which you do not understand. Most chess players do not guard their secrets jealously, (though some are not so good at explaining how they do what they do), but, in general, they will be only too pleased to make use of any opportunity of testing or showing off their skill. Simply watching two expert players go over a game in the analysis room can be an education in itself.

(9) *Chess books*. It is a well-known fact that there are more books published on chess than on all other sports and games put together. We would again suggest that it is a good idea to ask an experienced hand about what is, and what is not, a good buy amongst this mountain of confusion. Many younger players will rush out and invest money on the latest edition of hard-core analysis on the "Perspiration System", only to discover later that the book is almost totally useless for their purposes. If you are going to buy opening books, and you will need some, then we suggest you concentrate on those which devote a little space to the written word and the explanation of various ideas behind the moves. Many of the younger British writers are good on this; Hartston, Pritchett, Stean, Nunn, and Keene (especially in his earlier work), amongst others, are worth investigating; but many wordless theoretical works are a waste of time for anyone under master strength. Also, there are certain writers who are well worth avoiding.

(10) *Gamesmanship*. Fischer used to say that he liked "to crush the other guy's ego" and made headlines in the world press as much through his off-the-board antics as through his brilliant play. Sometimes the struggle in a chess game is not restricted to over-the-board moves — we all know certain players who are compulsive

"j'adoubers", "shakers", "piece-bangers", etc. We would recommend Hartston's *How to Cheat at Chess* for a light-hearted and illuminating study of this seamy side of chess and hope that it does not occur too much in your own games. How one uses, or chooses to react to, gamesmanship is very much a personal matter which we must leave to the reader's own discretion. And with these final words we take leave of you. We wish you well, yet renounce all responsibility by saying that:

The rest is up to you!

SOLUTIONS TO EXERCISES: Lessons 1–4.
Tactics and Combinations

1. 1 Rxe6 Rxe6 2 Qg6+! Rxg6 3 hxg6+ Kh8 4 Nf7 mate.
2. 1 Qf8+ Bg8 2 Qf6+! Bxf6 3 Bxf6 mate.
3. 1 ... Rg2!!
4. 1 Rxf7 Rxf7 2 Rf1 Rf8 3 g6 hxg6 4 g5. Zugzwang. After Black's queen-side pawns have expended their moves, Black must lose a piece.
5. 1 a4! Bxa4 2 Qa3 Bb5 3 Rxb5 Qxa3 4 Rb7+ and 5 bxa3.
6. 1 Bb8!! White wins material.
7. 1 Be7! Bxe7 2 Qe5+ f6 3 Qe6 and 4 Qf7.
8. 1 ... Ng3+! 2 hxg3 hxg3+ 3 Kg1 Nf2 4 Rxf2 Rh1+! 5 Kxh1 gxf2. Nothing can stop the pawn.
9. 1 Rxh2! gxh2 2 Bb1 h1=Q/R stalemate. ½–½.
10. 1 Qxd8+! Bxd8 2 Bxb7. Not an everyday back-rank combination.
11. 1 ... Kd4! Zugzwang. 2 Be1 (2 Be3+ Kc3 and 3 ... Kb2) ... Rxe1+! 3 Kxe1 Kc3 4 Ra1 Kb2 5 Rd1 Bxd1 with an easily won ending.
12. 1 ... Qh3 2 Re2 Qxg3+! 3 hxg3 Nxe2+ 4 Kf2 Nxc1 5 Rxc1 Rc8, another example of a winning pin (see position 4) if 6 b3 then 6 ... Rd2+. Or 6 Ke2 Rc4.
13. 1 ... Rc5!
14. 1 Qg7+ Kf8 2 Qh8+! Qf8 3 Qe5+ Re7 4 Bb5+! axb5 5 Qxb5+ Rdd7 6 Qb8+ perpetual check.
15. 1 Rf8+ Rxf8 2 Qh8!+ Kxh8 3 exf8(Q) mate.
16. 1 Bxf7+! Kxf7 2 Rxc7+ and Qh7+.
17. 1 Rxc8 Qxc8 2 Qxc8+ Kxc8 3 Rxf6 gxf6 4 g7 Be6 5 Bh3 and the pawn promotes.
18. 1 Rxh7+! Kxf7 2 Rxf7+ Rxf7 3 Qxg6+ and Qxf7.
19. 1 Qxc8+! Qxc8 2 Bc7 and Black cannot prevent Rxc8+ and Bd8.
20. 1 ... Nd7! forcing a positional concession from White with 2 d5. If 2 Ne2? Nde5! 3 dxe5 Nxe5 and 4 ... Nxd3+.
21. 1 Rxd7! Qxd7 2 Bxc6 Qc7 3 Bxa8 Rxa8 4 Qc6! White wins material.
22. 1 Nxe7+ Kh8. (1 ... Rxe7 2 Rhg1+ Kf7 3 Qg7+ and Qxe7 mate) 2 Qf8+ (or Qxh7+) Rxf8 3 Rxh7+ and Rh1 mate.
23. 1 Rg4+! fxg4 2 Qg5+ Kh8 3 Qh6 and the double mates (Qxf8 and Qxh7) prove decisive.
24. 1 ... Rh8!! This mysterious rook move comes from a Pachman game. White has no answer to the threat of 2 ... g6 3 Qxh6+ Kg8 winning the queen.
25. 1 Nf5+! gxf5 2 gxf5+ Kh7 3 Kf2!! allowing the rook on f1 access to the g-file and taking part in the attack! 3 ... Rg7 the best try at organizing a defence to Rg6 4 Qxh6+! 4 ... Kxh6 5 Rh3+ Kg5 6 Rg1+ Kf4 7 Rh4+ and mates.
26. 1 Qe8+! Rxe8 2 Nf7+ Nxf7 3 Rxe8 mate.
27. 1 ... Rxg2?? intending to answer 2 Qxf8+ with the cute ... Rg8+ and Rxf8. 2 Qxh7+ with stalemate! Correct is 1 ... Rf7 and Black has a comfortable win.
28. 1 Rxf7+! Kxf7 2 Qd7+ Kf6 3 Qd8+ Kg7 4 Qd7+ Kg8 5 Qc8+! Kh7 6 Qxb7+ Qg7 7 Qxh+. ½–½.
29. 1 Nh6+ Kf8 2 Nf5! e/gxf5 3 Rxh7 mating.
30. 1 Nxf5 Rxf5 2 Bxc7+! Kxc7 3 g4 winning the exchange.
31. 1 Qg7+! Kxg7 2 Nf5+ Kg8 3 Ne7 mate.
32. 1 Ra7+! Kxa7 2 Nc6+ Ka8 3 Qxb8+ Qxb8 4 Rxb8 mate.
33. 1 ... Re3!! White is powerless against Nh3 and Qg1 mate.
34. 1 ... Rb1! 2 Qxb1 Nxe3+ 3 Kg1 Qxf3 and mates. This combination was missed by Botvinnik who, in time trouble, accepted a draw.
35. 1 Qxh6+! gxh6 2 Rg7+ Kh8 3 Bg8!
36. 1 Be4! a variation on the interference theme. 1 ... Rxe4 2 h3+ Kg3 3 Rf3 mate. Or 1 ... Bxe4 2 h3+ Kg3 3 Be1 mate.

GLOSSARY

1. Tactics and Combinations

1. *Zwischenzug* is German for "in-between-move". This is a move which is "slipped in" before a forced reply, e.g. 1 e4 e6 2 d4 d5 3 e5 c5 4 c3 Nc6 5 Nf3 Qb6 6 Bd3 cxd4 7 cxd4 Nxd4?? 8 Nxd4 Qxd4? 9 Bb5+ Bd7 and now White plays a zwischenzug with 10 Bxd7+ before capturing the black queen on d4.

2. *Desperado piece* is a piece that is lost but gives up its life in the most expensive manner. In the previous example the white bishop on b5 could be classed as a "desperado".

3. *Rabbit*: A weak player; other terms are fish, muppet, zombie, etc. These unkind terms are part of chess lore. There is never any malice suggested in the term other than it refers to a weak player.

4. A *Hanging* piece is one which is unprotected, though not necessarily under attack (and thus a potential tactical weakness).

2. How to Analyse a Position

1. The *Branching factor* (plausible moves) is the number of reasonable moves which must be considered at every turn of play. Typically, (for humans), this will be 6 or 7 in an ordinary middle-game position. In computer chess, it may be the number of legal moves in the position.

2. *Essential features* refers to the general overview of a position involving such factors as open or half-open files, pawn structure and piece activity. This may include tactical points such as pins or hanging pieces.

3. *A Forcing sequence* is a series of moves in which one player's responses are forced to avert immediate disaster.

4. The *Game tree* is the "tree" which represents the plausible moves from a given position in terms of nodes connected by arcs.

5. *Progressive deepening* is the process of rehashing and rechecking previously analysed variations and extending them in successive stages, which humans perform before deciding on a move.

6. A *Threat* is an immediate tactical move such as a capture, pin, fork, double-attack, etc.

3. How to Formulate a Plan

1. *Open file*: a file with no pawns on it.

2. *Half-open file*: one with pawn(s) of only one colour on it.

3. *Isolated pawn*: a pawn with no friendly pawns on adjacent files.

4. *Hanging pawns* two pawns on the same rank on adjacent files with no friendly pawns on neighbouring files.

5. *Backward pawn*: a pawn which cannot be defended by another pawn, cannot advance without the risk of being taken by an enemy pawn, and is exposed to attack on a half-open file.

6. *Doubled pawns* are two pawns of the same colour on the same file, classed as a weakness because they cannot defend each other and an opposing single pawn can block them.

7. *Colour complex*: a group of undefended squares of one colour, arising from the pawn structure.

4. Opening Principles and Ideas

1. The *Opening* is the initial phase of the game in which the pieces are mobilized.

2. To *Centralize* is to move a piece towards the centre.

3. A *Power differential* is the difference in activity of the white and black pieces in a given position.

4. A *Fianchetto* is the development of a bishop on b2 or g2 for White, or on b7 or g7 for Black.

5. The *Two bishops* is a case of 1+1=2 and a little bit more, as a single bishop's inherent disadvantage of colour blindness is eliminated. In an open position, possession of the two bishops vs. (B + N) or (N + N) will normally give a definite positional advantage.

5. The Ending

1. The *Ending* is the phase of the game which is characterized by the paucity of material on the board and a general absence of complications typical of opening or middlegame positions.

2. *P.P.P.* is an abbreviation for protected passed pawn.

3. *D.P.P.* is an abbreviation for distant passed pawn.

4. *Zugzwang* is a German word with the literal meaning of "compulsion to move". The option of moving is not always an advantage and this is used in the sense of being forced to move and LOSE.

5. *Wrong bishop*: with relevance to the ending of king, bishop and rook pawn vs. king if the bishop does not control the queening square and the opposing king has access to that square, the bishop is said to be of the "wrong" colour as the enemy king cannot be forced out of the corner.